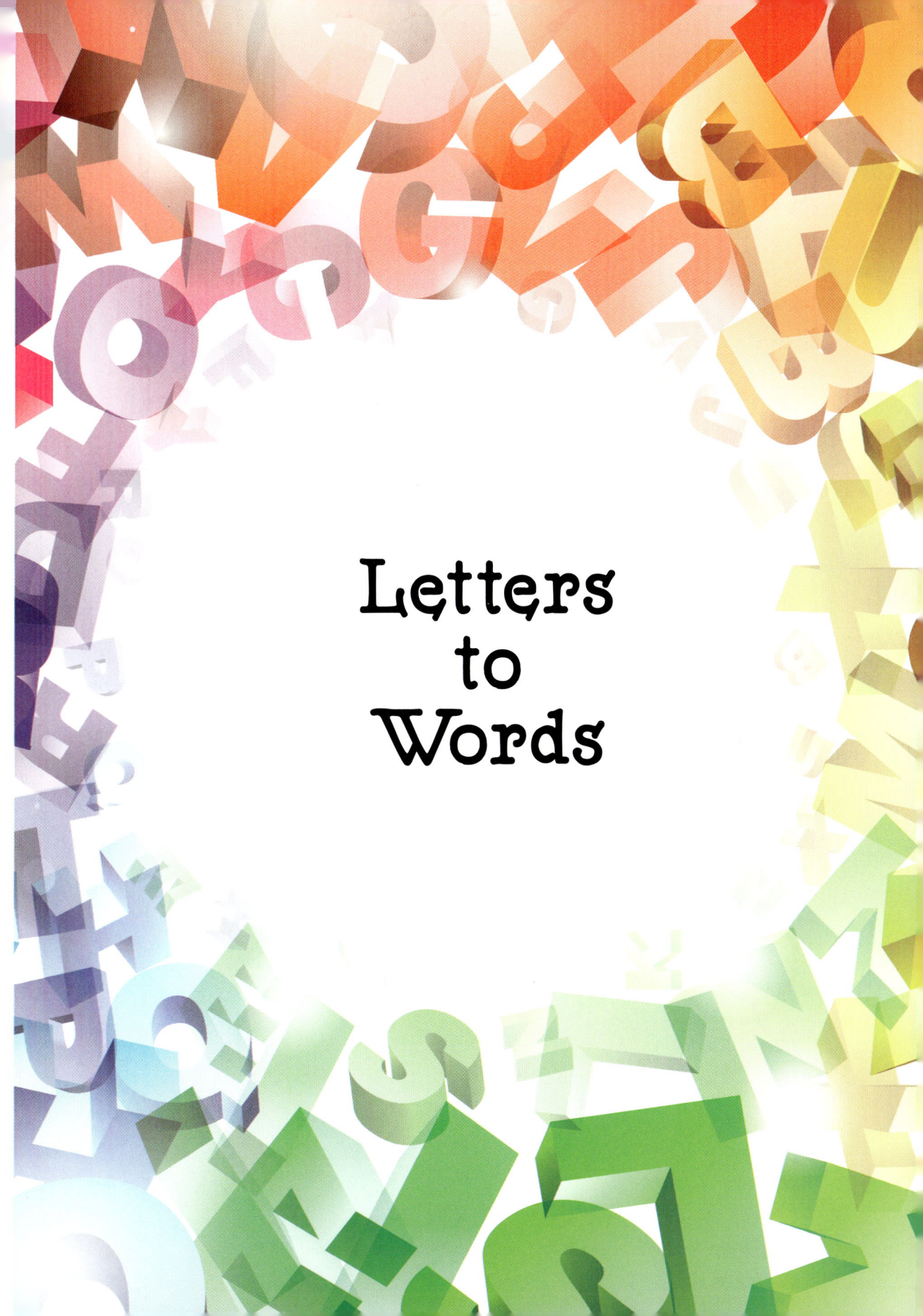

Letters to Words

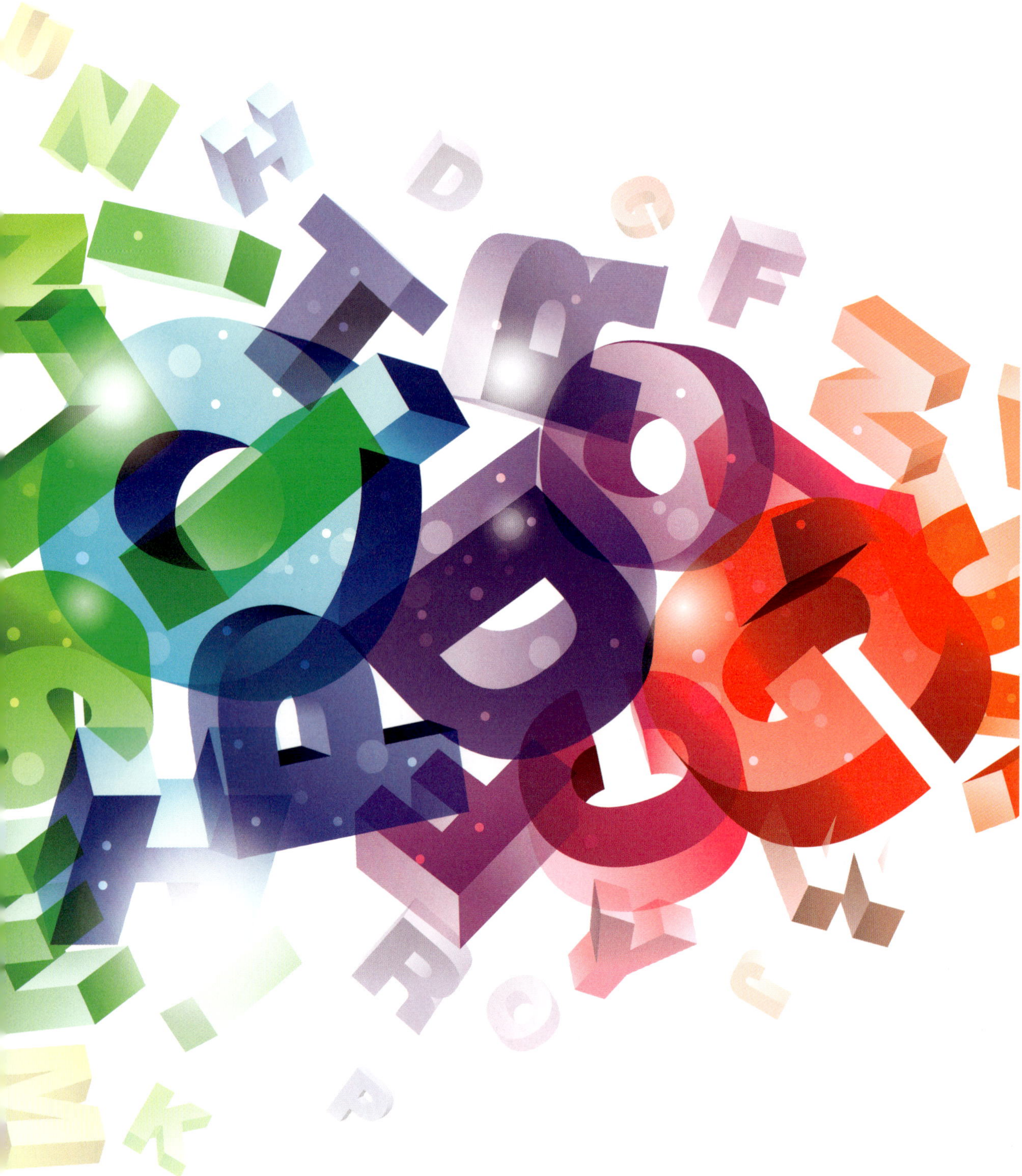

Letters to Words

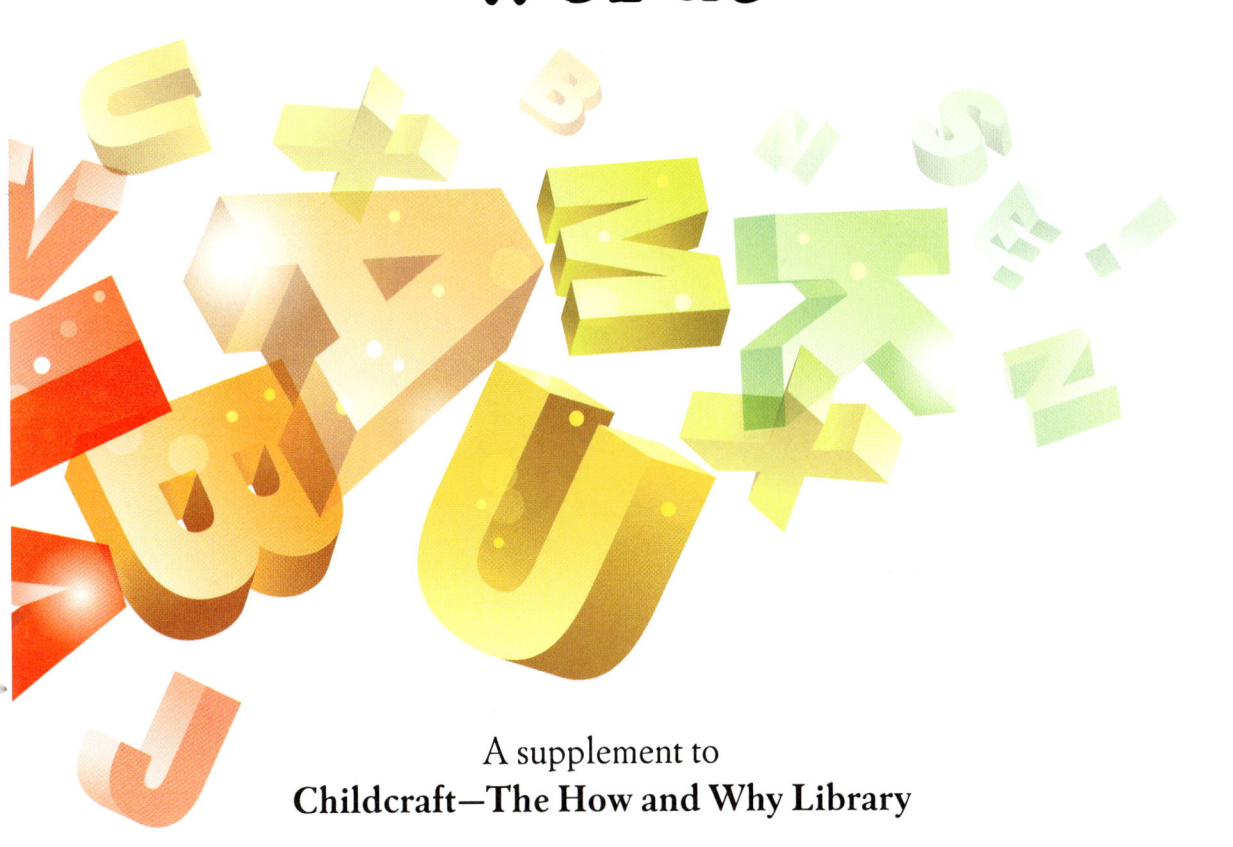

A supplement to
Childcraft—The How and Why Library

World Book, Inc.
a Scott Fetzer company
Chicago
www.worldbook.com

Staff

Executive Committee

President
  Donald D. Keller

Vice President and Editor in Chief
  Paul A. Kobasa

Vice President, Marketing &
  Digital Development
  Sean Klunder

Vice President, International
  Richard Flower

Controller
  Yan Chen

Director, Human Resources
  Bev Ecker

Editorial

Associate Director,
  Supplementary Publications
  Scott Thomas

Managing Editor,
  Supplementary Publications
  Barbara A. Mayes

Senior Editor
  Kristina Vaicikonis

Researcher
  Annie Brodsky

Administrative Assistant
  Ethel Matthews

Manager, Indexing Services
  David Pofelski

Manager, Contracts & Compliance
  (Rights & Permissions)
  Loranne K. Shields

Editorial Administration

Director, Systems and Projects
  Tony Tills

Senior Manager,
  Publishing Operations
  Timothy Falk

Associate Manager,
  Publishing Operations
  Audrey Casey

Manufacturing/Production

Director
  Carma Fazio

Manufacturing Manager
  Steven K. Hueppchen

Production/Technology Manager
  Anne Fritzinger

Production Specialist
  Curley Hunter

Proofreader
  Emilie Schrage

Graphics and Design

Senior Manager
  Tom Evans

Coordinator, Design Development
  and Production
  Brenda B. Tropinski

Photographs Editor
  Kathy Creech

Marketing

Director, Direct Marketing
  Mark R. Willy

Marketing Analyst
  Zofia Kulik

For information about other World Book publications, visit our website at www.worldbook.com or call 1-800-WORLDBK (967-5325). For information about sales to schools and libraries, call 1-800-975-3250 (United States), or 1-800-837-5365 (Canada).

© 2012 World Book, Inc. All rights reserved. This volume may not be reproduced in whole or in part in any form without prior written permission from the publisher.

CHILDCRAFT, CHILDCRAFT—THE HOW AND WHY LIBRARY, and the GLOBE DEVICE are registered trademarks or trademarks of World Book, Inc.

Library of Congress Cataloging-in-Publication Data

Letters to words : a supplement to Childcraft, the how and why library.
    p. cm.
  Includes index.
  Summary: "An introduction to letters and words, including information about how alphabets and writing systems developed, the meanings of names and everyday words, and the history of the English language. Features include stories from world literature, puzzles, and a list of additional resources"--Provided by publisher.
  ISBN 978-0-7166-0627-7
  1. Vocabulary--Juvenile literature. I. World Book, Inc. II. Childcraft.
PE1449.L4248 2012
428.1--dc23
                            2011049652

World Book, Inc.
233 N. Michigan Ave.
Chicago, IL 60601
Printed in the United States of America
by RR Donnelley, Willard, Ohio
1st Printing May 2012

Contents

Preface 7

From Sounds to Letters 8
    The story of the invention of writing and the alphabet

There's a Hippo in the Attic
    Eating a Sandwich 74
    Stories of the origins of many everyday words

What's in a Name? 106
    The meanings of many first and last names

How English Came to Be 124
    The story of how the English language came to be
    and how it has grown and changed over time

All Kinds of English 176
    Different ways of speaking, writing, and pronouncing
    English in various parts of the world

Fun with Words 186
    Riddles, puzzles, and word games

Find Out More 202

Index 204

Acknowledgments

The publishers of *Childcraft—The How and Why Library* gratefully acknowledge the courtesy of the following individuals and agencies for illustrations in this volume. When all the illustrations for a sequence of pages are from a single source, the inclusive page numbers are given. Credits should be read left to right, top to bottom, on their respective pages. All illustrations are the exclusive property of World Book, Inc. unless otherwise noted.

Covers
Aristocrat, Discovery, and Standard Bindings: Alice Feagan
Heritage Binding: © Peter Horree, Alamy Images; © Shutterstock; Shutterstock; © Shutterstock; Jerry Pinkney; Alice Feagan; © iStockphoto; Alice Feagan; © Shutterstock; © Shutterstock
Rainbow Binding: © Shutterstock; © Shutterstock; © Shutterstock; © The Print Collector/Alamy Images; © Shutterstock; © Shutterstock; © Dreamstime

Illustrations

1-7	© Shutterstock
8-9	Alice Feagan
10-11	Jerry Pinkney; © Réunion des Musées Nationaux/Art Resource; WORLD BOOK photos
12-13	Jerry Pinkney; WORLD BOOK photo; © Shutterstock; © Peter Horree, Alamy Images
14-15	© Bridgeman Art Library; © age fotostock/SuperStock
16-23	Brian Froud
24-25	© Shutterstock; © iStockphoto
26-27	Jerry Pinkney
28-29	© SuperStock/Alamy Images
30-31	Semitic Museum, Harvard University
32-33	Jerry Pinkney; © Alinari Archives/Getty Images
34-35	Jerry Pinkney
36-37	© Dreamstime; © DeAgostini/SuperStock; Jerry Pinkney; © Shutterstock
38-39	© Michael Juno, Alamy Images; © Shutterstock
40-41	© Giraudon/Bridgeman Art Library
42-44	Jerry Pinkney
44-45	© Shutterstock
46-69	Robert Byrd
74-75	Alice Feagan
76-79	Phillip Wende; © Shutterstock
80-81	Jerry Pinkney; © Shutterstock; © Dreamstime
82-83	© Shutterstock; Tom Dolan; Jerry Pinkney
84-85	© Dreamstime; Jerry Pinkney; © Ingram Publishing/Thinkstock
86-87	© Shutterstock
88-89	Jerry Pinkney; © Shutterstock
90-91	Phillip Wende; © Shutterstock
92-93	Phillip Wende; © iStockphoto
94-95	© David R. Frazier Photolibrary/Alamy Images; © Dennis Hallinan/Alamy Images; © iStockphoto
96-99	Phillip Wende
98	© Shutterstock
100-103	Phillip Wende; © Shutterstock
106-107	Alice Feagan
108-111	© Shutterstock
112-123	Phillip Wende
124-125	Alice Feagan
126-131	Max Ranft
132-133	Paul Williams; Brian Froud
134-137	Brian Froud
138-143	Max Ranft
144-146	Paul Williams
146-153	Ronald LeHew
154-161	Lydia Halverson; Kinuko Craft
162-163	Max Ranft; © Shutterstock
164-165	Shutterstock; Kinuko Craft
166-173	Kinuko Craft
174-175	Robert Masheris
176-177	Alice Feagan
178-179	© Shutterstock
180-181	© Mary Evans Picture Library
182-185	John Magine; © Shutterstock
186-187	Alice Feagan
188-189	Dave and Shirley Beckes; © Shutterstock
190-191	Dave and Shirley Beckes
192-193	Sharon Elzuardia; © Shutterstock; © iStockphoto
194-195	Sharon Elzuardia
208	Robert Byrd

The publishers of *Childcraft—The How and Why Library* gratefully acknowledge the courtesy of the following publishers for permission to use copyrighted material in this volume:

Page 180, "Waltzing Matilda," Copyright © 1936 Allans & Co. Copyright © 1941 Carl Fischer, Inc. Copyright renewed. All rights assigned to Carl Fischer, LLC. All rights reserved. Used by permission.

Preface

Letters are amazing! By itself, a single letter may not mean much. But put them together, and letters become words.

Say the word *dog*. That word is just a noise that you make with your tongue and throat. But any speaker of English who hears it will think of a furry, four-footed animal that barks and wags its tail. So, with nothing but a noise, you can put a picture of a dog in other people's minds. Words are pretty amazing!

With words, people can share ideas and knowledge and fun, both directly and through time. No other creature on Earth can do such things. Only human beings have the power of words.

Did you ever wonder where these noises we call letters and words came from—how they began? Letters were invented by people who lived long ago. Many of the words you use come from long ago, too. Most of them have stories to tell. They've been through many adventures. You use words that sailed with the hardy Vikings and rode with the armored knights of Normandy. You use words that were made up by Greek explorers in Egypt thousands of years ago. There's a tale behind most words—a tale that may be funny, surprising, or exciting.

Read on, and find out about these wonderful things called letters and words. Find out what some of the words you use really mean—why you call a certain kind of dog a *poodle*, and why the top of a house is called a *roof*. Find out what names mean, for names are words, too. Discover the fascinating tale of how writing came to be and the marvelous adventure story of the English language. Find out the many ways you can use words for fun and entertainment. You're in for a real treat!

From Sounds to Letters

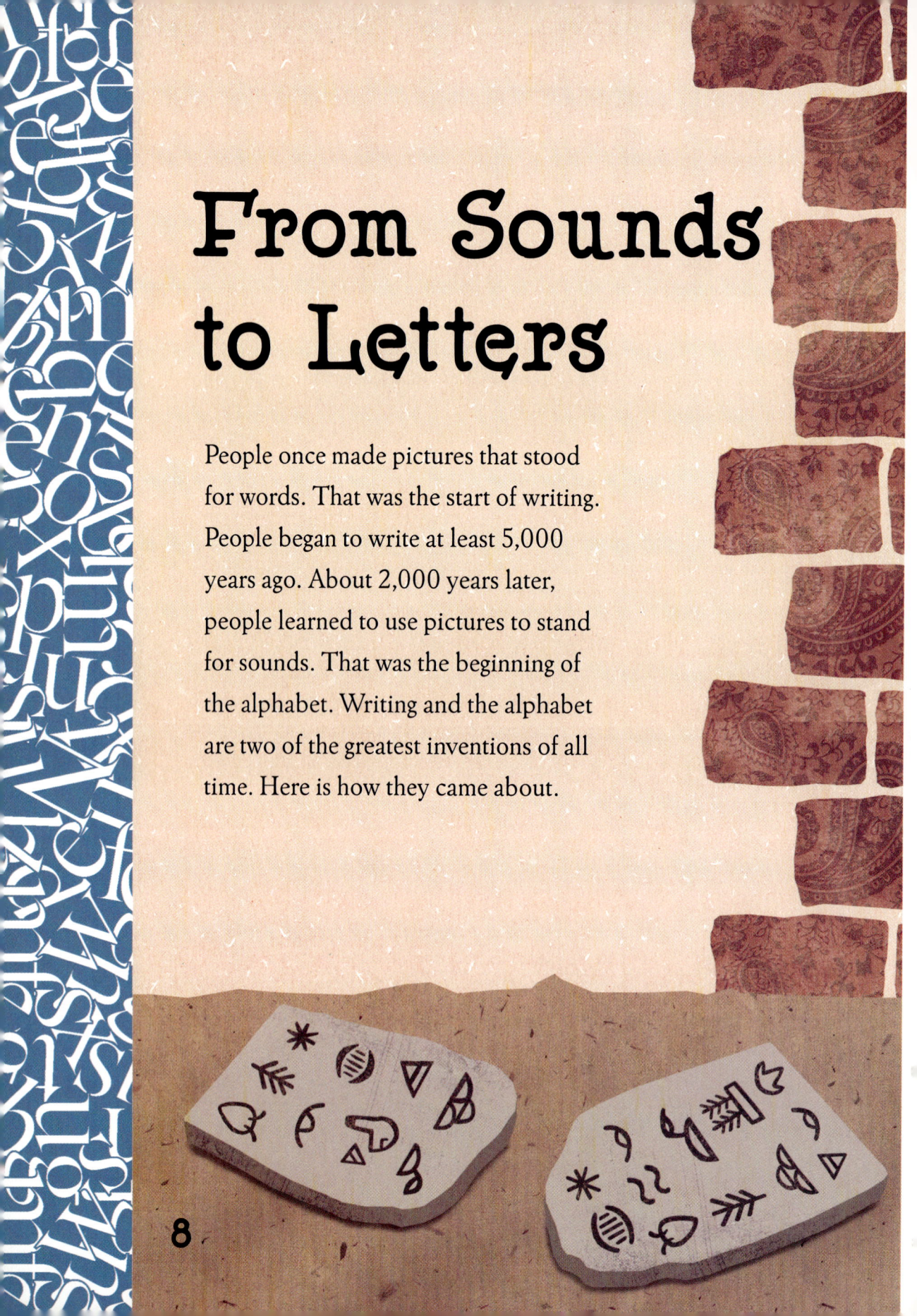

People once made pictures that stood for words. That was the start of writing. People began to write at least 5,000 years ago. About 2,000 years later, people learned to use pictures to stand for sounds. That was the beginning of the alphabet. Writing and the alphabet are two of the greatest inventions of all time. Here is how they came about.

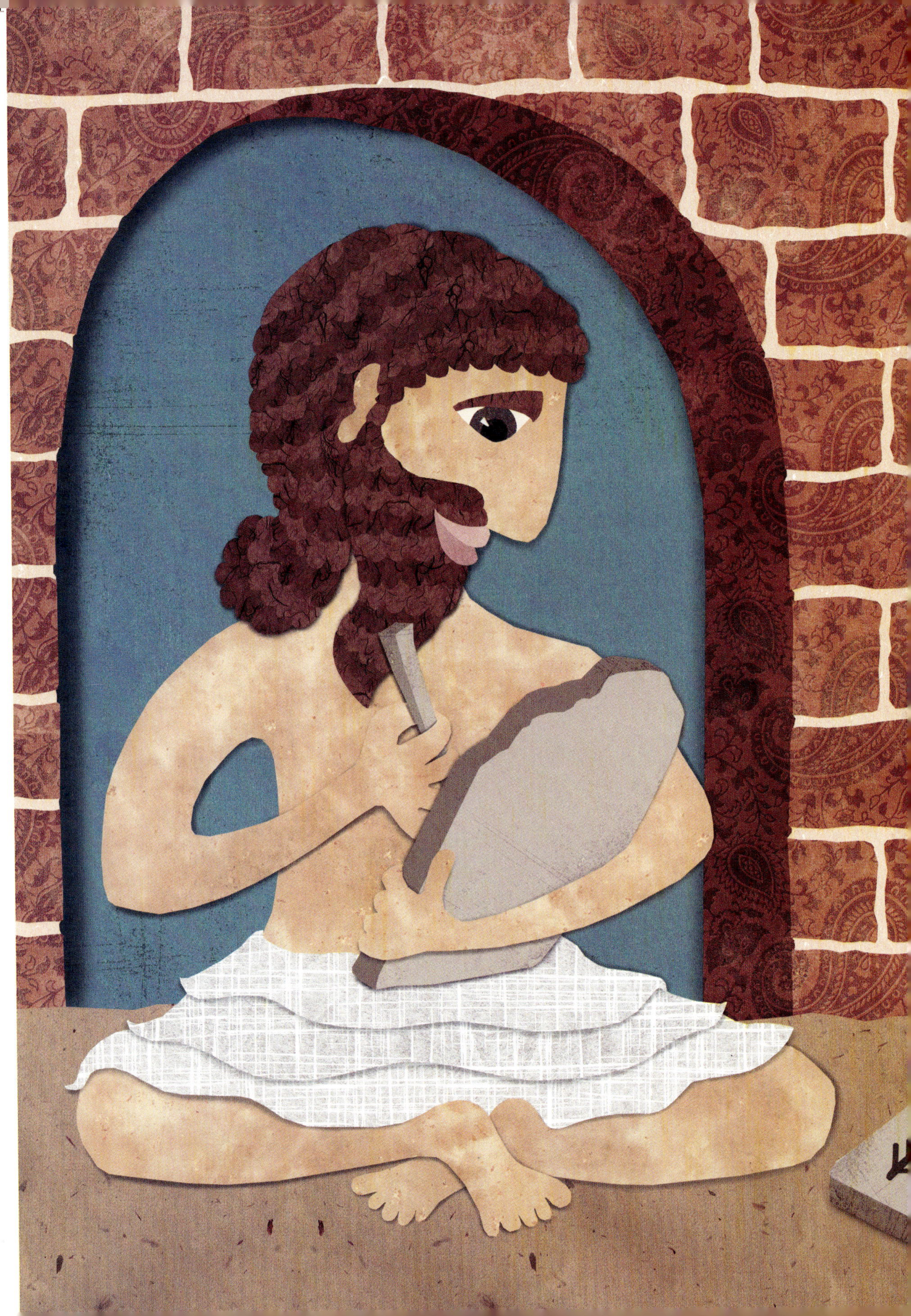

Marks in mud

We didn't always have writing. For hundreds of thousands of years, the only way people could pass ideas along was by talking. There was no way to write stories or keep written records. So people had to do a lot of remembering.

Then, some 5,000 years ago, in a hot land in the Middle East, someone had a wonderful idea. Pictures could be used to stand for spoken words. With rows of pictures that stood for words, people could preserve stories, send letters to each other, and keep historical and business records.

Pictures that stand for words are called pictograms. This word simply means "picture writing." The first people to use pictograms were the Sumerians, who lived in what today is southeastern Iraq. The Sumerians must have had a hard time finding pictures for some of their words. It's easy to turn such a word as *fish, bird,* or *house* into a picture—you just draw a picture of a fish, a bird, or a house. But it's not so easy to find pictures for such words as *here, understand,* or *good.* Try it and see.

The Sumerians solved this problem by putting different pictures together to mean certain words. For example, their picture for the word *food* was a bowl, because they ate out of bowls. When they put a picture of a head next to a tilted bowl, it meant *eat.* But there is a big problem with this kind of writing. You need

Sumerian picture writing from about 4,300 years ago

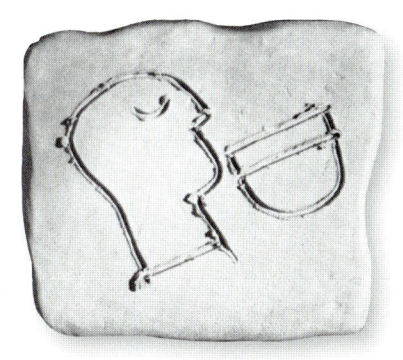

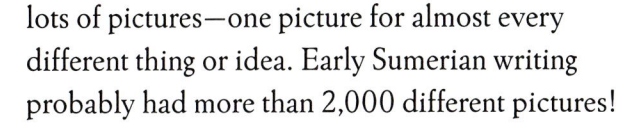

The Sumerian symbol for the word "eat" was a head beside a food bowl.

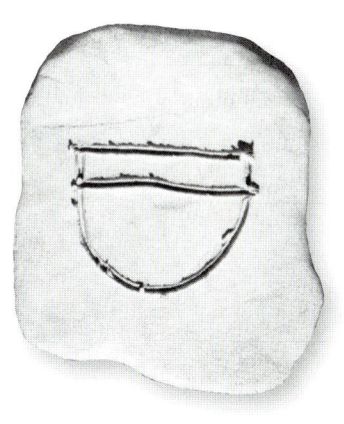

The Sumerian symbol for the word "food" was a bowl.

lots of pictures—one picture for almost every different thing or idea. Early Sumerian writing probably had more than 2,000 different pictures!

The Sumerians made their pictures with sharp sticks in flat lumps of clay. This clay wasn't like the modeling clay you use. It was more like thick, stiff mud. The clay tablets were covered with pictures and then baked or dried in the sun. This hardened the clay.

If you have tried to draw pictures in clay, you know it isn't easy. It's especially hard to draw curves. The lines get filled in, and the edges get squeezed up. This happened to the pictures the Sumerians made on their clay tablets. But because clay was the best thing the Sumerians had to write on, that is what they used.

From Sounds to Letters

Over time, Sumerian writing grew more abstract, that is, less real or concrete. the word "fish" (above, top), which once looked like a fish, ended up looking nothing like a fish (above, bottom).

After a time, the Sumerians found that it was easier to draw only straight lines. So they began to make all their picture words out of straight lines. For example, the word *fish* was first a picture of a fish made with curved lines. Then it was made with straight lines. Finally, it became a bunch of straight lines that didn't look like a fish at all. Then it was no longer a picture word. It was a symbol that stood for a word. All the Sumerian writing became symbols that stood for words or parts of words.

12 Letters to Words

← Sumerian cuneiform writing on clay tablets was made with small, sharp sticks. The marks were wedge-shaped, which is how the writing got its name; the word "cuneiform" means "wedge-shaped."

The way the Sumerians pushed their little sticks into the clay caused the marks to look like golf tees. So, instead of being all straight lines, the Sumerian writing began to look like designs made with golf tees.

This kind of writing is called cuneiform, which means "wedge-shaped." For more than 2,000 years, the cuneiform writing started by the Sumerians was used by Assyrians, Babylonians, and other people in the same part of the Middle East.

About 20,000 cuneiform tablets have been found in what is now Iraq. They were written in a language called Akkadian, which began to replace Sumerian as the official language in some parts of the region 3,600 years ago or earlier.

From Sounds to Letters   **13**

The language detective

How is it that we are able to read the strange-looking cuneiform writing of the Sumerians? No one has spoken their language for thousands of years. How can a language be read if no one knows what the symbols mean?

We learned this language mainly through the work of a man who studied and puzzled and put clues together until he figured out how to read cuneiform writing. His name was Henry Rawlinson.

Rawlinson was a British army officer. In 1835, he was on duty in Persia, which is now called Iran. While there, he visited Behistun Rock, a mountain cliff in Kermanshah province. High up on this rock, there is an ancient carving of a king, his servants, and a group of prisoners. And there are three different kinds of ancient cuneiform writing.

Rawlinson copied the cuneiform inscriptions and began to study them. He realized that one of them was in a language much like an East Indian language that he could speak and write. Slowly, he worked out the meaning of this inscription, which was in ancient Persian. It told of the military deeds of Darius, king of Persia.

Letters to Words

Rawlinson then found that the names of some kings in the Persian inscription seemed to be repeated in the other inscriptions. Perhaps all three inscriptions said the same thing! Using the Persian inscription as a key, Rawlinson was able to puzzle out the meaning of the symbols in the other inscriptions. Thanks to the work of Rawlinson and others, we are now able to read the cuneiform writing invented in ancient Sumer.

← A stone carving on a cliff called the Behistun Rock in what is now Iran celebrates the victory of Darius, king of Persia, over several rebel kings about 2,500 years ago.

Darius had the history of his family engraved in cuneiform writing above and below the figures.
↓

From Sounds to Letters

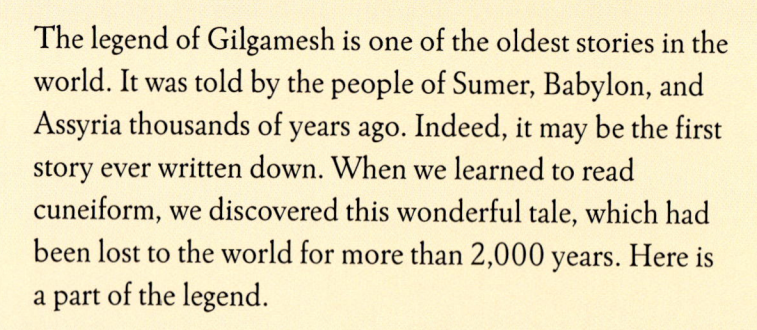

The legend of Gilgamesh is one of the oldest stories in the world. It was told by the people of Sumer, Babylon, and Assyria thousands of years ago. Indeed, it may be the first story ever written down. When we learned to read cuneiform, we discovered this wonderful tale, which had been lost to the world for more than 2,000 years. Here is a part of the legend.

The Journey of Gilgamesh

In the land of Sumer, in the city of Uruk, there lived two great and mighty warriors. One was Prince Gilgamesh, son of Queen Ninsun. The other was Gilgamesh's dearest friend and constant companion, Enkidu.

Gilgamesh was a happy, carefree young man. But one day he awakened filled with gloom. He spent most of the day deep in thought. Then he went to see his friend.

"Enkidu," he said, "all men die, and someday I, too, will die and be gone from the world forever. My name will be forgotten. It will be as if I had never been! I cannot let this happen. I must do something to make my name live on. So, I am going to the Mountain of the Cedar Forest that is the home of the evil monster Humbaba. I will challenge the monster to fight me. When I have killed him, I will put my name on a stone and set the stone on the mountaintop."

From Sounds to Letters

Enkidu raised his hands in alarm. "You do not know what a terrible creature this Humbaba is!" he cried. "His breath is fire and a whirlwind! His footsteps are earthquakes! The gaze of his eye turns men to stone!"

"What does it matter?" argued Gilgamesh. "If I am to die anyway, I may as well die battling this creature. Then, men will always remember that I died bravely!"

Enkidu sighed. "I will go with you, of course," he told his friend. "But I beg of you to pray to Shamash the sun god and ask for his help."

So Gilgamesh prayed to the sun god, telling him what he planned to do and asking his help.

"When you are in need, I will help you," whispered the voice of Shamash.

Then Gilgamesh and Enkidu went to the metalworkers and had their swords and axes sharpened. When the wise men who governed the city of Uruk heard of Gilgamesh's plan, they raised their hands in horror and pleaded with him not to go. His mother, Ninsun the queen, wept and wrung her hands. She, too, prayed to Shamash to protect her son and help him come safely back.

Gilgamesh and Enkidu set out. For many days they traveled. They crossed mountains and made their way through dark forests that seemed to go on forever. But at last they reached the foot of the Mountain of Cedars. It rose above them, tall and awesome, its peak lost in the clouds.

Then Gilgamesh grasped his ax and with several blows brought one of the trees crashing to the ground. The sound of its falling echoed on the mountainside.

Far up in the cedar forest, there was a terrible roaring, like the sound of a whirlwind. Out of his house of cedar logs stalked the monster Humbaba. He was taller than three men, with arms and legs as thick as tree trunks and great claws on his fingers and toes. His mouth was filled with sharp teeth. In the middle of his forehead was one eye, the eye whose glare could turn men to stone.

The ground shook and the cedar trees shuddered as the monster strode down the mountainside. Gilgamesh and Enkidu gripped their weapons and waited.

Humbaba burst out of the trees and bent his head to look down upon the two men and turn them to stone. But at that moment, burning winds and a fierce brightness came out of the sky and struck Humbaba's eye so that he howled with pain and covered his eye with his hand. The sun god, Shamash, was helping Gilgamesh in his time of need, as he had promised.

Gilgamesh and Enkidu leaped to the attack. They slashed the monster's legs so that he tumbled to the ground, and they cut off his head. Then Gilgamesh and Enkidu returned to Uruk in triumph.

The goddess Ishtar, who had seen the terrible battle, fell in love with the handsome Gilgamesh. Appearing beside him, she put her hand on his arm and smiled at him. "Gilgamesh," she said, "be my husband! Marry me. As a wedding present, I will give you a chariot made of gold and covered with jewels. I will enchant your horses so that they are the swiftest and your oxen so that they are the strongest. I will make all the kings and rulers of the world bow down before you!"

Ishtar was gloriously beautiful, but Gilgamesh frowned and shook off her hand. "If I marry you, what will become of me?" he asked, quietly. "It is known, oh Ishtar, that you have had many husbands. When you tire of one, you turn him into a dog or a snake! Why should I let such a thing happen to me? No, I will not marry you."

From Sounds to Letters **21**

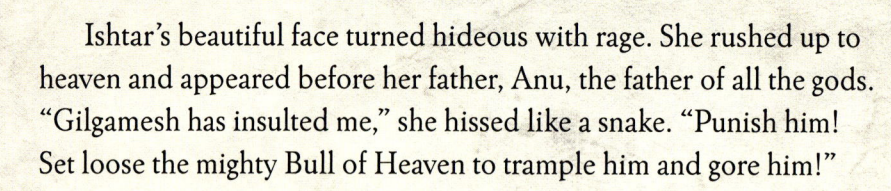

Ishtar's beautiful face turned hideous with rage. She rushed up to heaven and appeared before her father, Anu, the father of all the gods. "Gilgamesh has insulted me," she hissed like a snake. "Punish him! Set loose the mighty Bull of Heaven to trample him and gore him!"

"If I let loose the Bull of Heaven, terrible things will happen to the world of men," Anu warned. "There will be storms of wind, raging floods, and starvation."

"I will hold back the winds and floods, and see that the people do not starve," shrieked Ishtar, "but I want Gilgamesh punished! Set loose the Bull!"

So Anu loosed the Bull. It came rushing down out of heaven, bellowing with the sound of thunder and shaking its horns so that lightning flashed. The breath from its nose sent whirlwinds rushing before it, and the force of its hoofs made the earth shudder with earthquakes as it smashed the gates of Uruk.

But when the Bull charged at the two heroes, Enkidu seized it by the horns and held it still while Gilgamesh buried his ax in its neck and killed it.

Ishtar appeared again. "Woe to you, Gilgamesh!" she shrieked. "You have insulted me and killed the mighty Bull of Heaven. I will have vengeance upon you!"

The two friends simply laughed at her. They cut up the Bull and divided it among the people. Then Gilgamesh went to give thanks to the sun god.

Pictures on paper

The Sumerians preserved stories and kept records in cuneiform. At the same time, people in other parts of the Middle East and Asia were also developing ways of writing.

The people of ancient Egypt invented a kind of picture writing we call hieroglyphics. This name means "sacred carvings." The Greeks gave it this name because they thought the Egyptian priests were the only ones who used and understood this kind of writing.

Ancient Egyptian hieroglyphics painted on stone

Egyptian picture writing is very different from the picture writing of the Sumerians. Egyptian hieroglyphics are detailed pictures of people, animals, birds, plants, and everyday things with which the Egyptians were familiar. In some cases, one picture stood for one thing or idea. In other cases, the pictures stood for words or parts of words.

The ancient Egyptians also gave the world something better to write on than clay: They invented paper. To make sheets of paper, they used the dried leaves of the papyrus plant. These plants grew thickly along the banks of the Nile, the great river that flowed through their land. The Egyptians left many records on sheets of papyrus paper. They also carved their hieroglyphics on stone monuments and painted them in bright colors on the walls of tombs and temples.

Hieroglyphics on a jar used to store such mummified organs as the stomach

Some Egyptian writing was in straight lines, as ours is. The Egyptians sometimes wrote from left to right. But they also wrote from right to left, like this:

.esuom a desahc tac ehT

And some Egyptian writing went from top to bottom as well as right to left, like this:

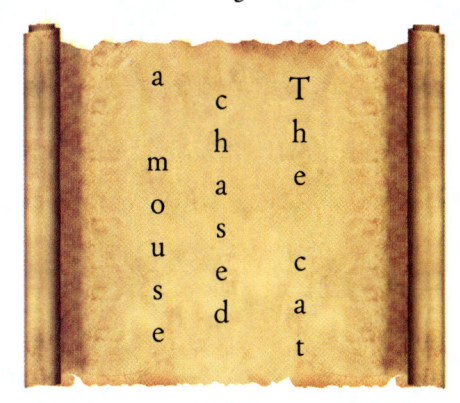

```
a    c    T
     h    h
m    a    e
o    s
u    e    c
s    d    a
e         t
```

From Sounds to Letters **25**

Words from ancient

When you set in the western horizon of heaven
The world is in darkness like the dead . . .
Every lion comes forth from his den
The serpents they sting. Darkness reigns . . .

Bright is the earth when you rise on the horizon . . .
The two lands are in daily rejoicing,
Awake and standing upon their feet . . .
Then in all the world they begin their work.

Letters to Words

Egypt

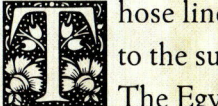

Those lines are from an ancient Egyptian hymn to the sun, written more than 3,000 years ago. The Egyptians wrote hymns, poems, and stories in their hieroglyphics. We can read these words from long ago because of the work of another language detective, Jean-François Champollion.

Champollion lived in France from 1790 to 1832. When he was 11 years old, someone showed him some Egyptian hieroglyphics and told him that no one in the world could read this ancient writing.

"I am going to do it!" the boy declared.

When he grew older, he studied all that was known about hieroglyphics. He made copies of hieroglyphic writing that had been found. He sorted out all the different kinds of pictures that were used in them. And he learned to speak several ancient languages.

From Sounds to Letters

In 1799, a French soldier in Egypt found a large stone slab with three kinds of writing carved on it. This stone was named the Rosetta stone. Some of the writing on it is in ancient Greek and some is in hieroglyphics.

Ancient Greek was one of the languages that Champollion had learned. When he saw the stone, he noticed that in the Greek writing, several names were repeated. Then he found some of the hieroglyphics were repeated in just the same way. Perhaps the Egyptian hieroglyphics said the same thing the Greek writing did. In time, he was able to match the hieroglyphics to the Greek. He had solved the mystery of Egyptian writing, just as he said he would!

The Rosetta stone, which is on display at the British Museum in London, provided the key that unlocked the lost meaning of Egyptian hieroglyphics.

Letters to Words

The wonderful invention

It takes us only a few seconds to write the words, "I wonder." But here's how an Egyptian wrote them:

One of the problems with both hieroglyphic and cuneiform writing was that it took a long time to write anything. Most words were made up of several pictures or symbols, and each one took time to draw.

Another difficulty was that hundreds of pictures or symbols were needed. The earliest cuneiform writing had about 600 symbols, and hieroglyphics also used several hundred symbols. In both kinds of writing, a symbol could stand for a word or a syllable. Only someone who had spent years learning the meanings of all these pictures and symbols—and how to make them—could write. It took so long to learn how to write, and the writing seemed so hard to do, that most people thought it was a kind of magic.

Semite letters on an ancient coin

Then, by 1500 B.C., came a wonderful invention—the alphabet! The people who had this great idea lived in a land of brown hills and palm trees, probably in the area where Egypt's Sinai Peninsula and Israel are today. We call these people Semites. They were probably slaves of the Egyptians, but their invention of the alphabet changed the world.

At first, the Semites probably used Egyptian writing, with its hundreds of pictures. But great thinkers among the Semites must have realized that a picture could stand for a single sound just as well as for a word or a syllable. They began to use some of the Egyptian symbols for sounds. This made it easier to write. Finally, they had 27 symbols that could be put together to make any word in their language. This was the beginning of the alphabet.

Eventually, some Semitic groups began to use an alphabet with 22 symbols. Each symbol was a picture of something and stood for the first sound in the name of the thing pictured. For example, a wavy line, which was a picture of water, was called *mem*, the Semitic word for water. But to the Semites the symbol *mem* didn't mean water. It stood for the first *m* sound in the word mem.

Letters to Words

Two of the symbols used by the Semites, an ox head and an eye, stood for scratchy, growly sounds we don't have in English. However, eventually, those symbols developed into our letters *a* and *o*. Several other symbols stood for sounds we make by putting two of our letters together, such as *ts* and *sh*. And all the Semitic letters stood for hard sounds such as *kuh* and *tuh*, the sounds we call consonants. The Semitic alphabet had no letters for sounds such as *ay*, *ee*, and *oh*, the sounds we call vowels.

Semitic alphabet

From Sounds to Letters **31**

The alphabet goes to sea

When the alphabet was invented, people called Phoenicians lived along the coast of what is now Israel and Syria. They were skillful sailors, brave explorers, talented *artisans* (people skilled in such trades as woodworking, metalworking, and weaving), and clever merchants. Their ships glided through the sparkling waters of the Mediterranean Sea, exploring the shores and islands. When the Phoenicians met people in their travels, they offered to trade brightly colored cloth, jewelry, and spices for whatever valuable things the people might have.

Letters to Words

Phoenician alphabet

The Phoenicians didn't live far from where the alphabet was invented, so they soon heard about this new way of writing. Before long, they began to use it themselves. They spoke much the same language as the inventors of the alphabet, so they didn't need to change any of the sounds the symbols stood for. But they did change the shapes of most of the symbols—perhaps to make them easier to write.

The Phoenicians took their new writing to sea with them, to use for keeping records of their business deals. Thus, the alphabet was carried to other lands.

Phoenician lettering on a stone found on the island of Sardinia in what is now Italy

From Sounds to Letters

New sounds and

The Phoenician traders often sailed across the Mediterranean Sea to a land of purple mountains and dark green groves of olive trees. This land was called Hellas by its people. Today, we call it Greece.

There is a legend that a Phoenician prince named Kadmus taught the Greeks the alphabet. But before the Greeks could use it, they had to make changes.

For one thing, the Phoenician language was nothing at all like the Greek language. Some sounds that the Phoenicians used were not used by the Greeks. For another thing, the Phoenician alphabet had only consonant sounds, but the Greeks needed seven vowel sounds. So the Greeks turned some of

34 Letters to Words

shapes

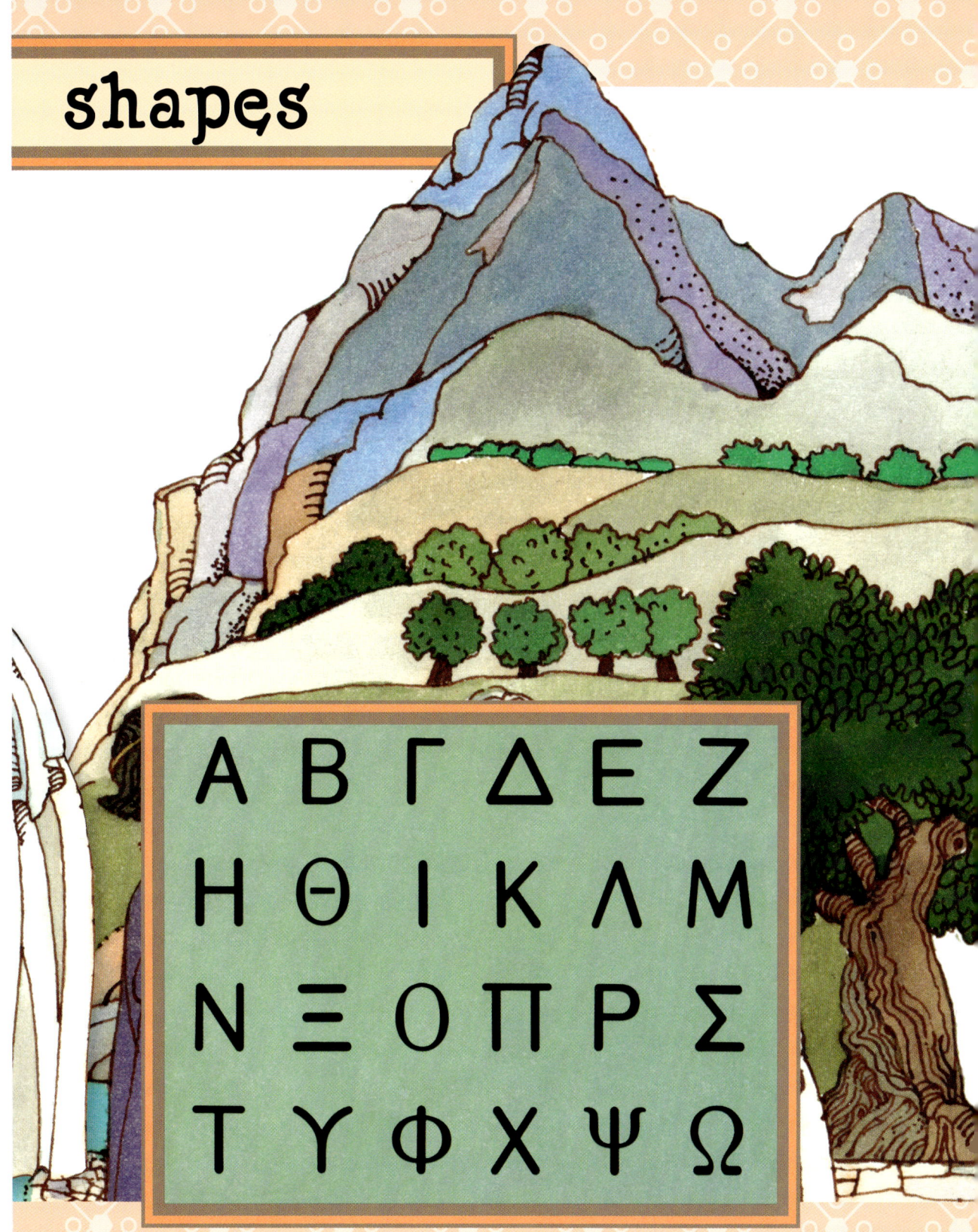

Α Β Γ Δ Ε Ζ
Η Θ Ι Κ Λ Μ
Ν Ξ Ο Π Ρ Σ
Τ Υ Φ Χ Ψ Ω

Greek alphabet

From Sounds to Letters   35

the Phoenician symbols for sounds the Greeks didn't use into the needed vowel letters. They also added several new symbols for new sounds and changed the shapes of many of the Phoenician symbols to ones they liked better.

The Greeks called the first two letters of their alphabet *alpha* and *beta*—and that's where our word *alphabet* comes from.

↑
Greek lettering carved in stone

Greek lettering on ancient pottery →

36   Letters to Words

More changes

Just as the Phoenician alphabet traveled to Greece, the Greek alphabet traveled to other places, too. About 2,700 years ago, a rich, powerful people called Etruscans ruled much of northern Italy. They used an alphabet much like the Greek alphabet, with a few changes to meet the needs of their language.

One of the places the Etruscans ruled was a simple farming community called Rome, whose people called themselves Romans. In time, the Romans rose up and drove out the Etruscans. But the Romans kept many of the good ideas they'd gotten from the Etruscans, such as architecture, religious ideas, and the alphabet.

From Sounds to Letters

↑ Roman lettering carved on a marble plaque near the entrance to the Colosseum in Rome

Roman lettering on a coin

38 Letters to Words

Over a period of time, the Romans, too, made changes in the alphabet. For one thing, they put in a letter that looked like our *v*, but they used it for both the vowel sound of *u* and the consonant sound of *w*. They didn't need a *zee* sound, so they took the letter *z* out. Later, they put it back in to use for foreign words. But they put it at the end of the alphabet.

The Romans also changed most of the Greek letters into shapes with neat, straight lines and curves. By about 2,000 years ago, their alphabet looked much like ours does now, except that it did not have the letters *j*, *u*, or *w*.

A B C D E F G
H I J K L M N
O P Q R S T
U V W X Y Z

Roman alphabet

Little letters

Rome began as a tiny village but grew to be a great city and the capital of a huge empire. The Romans conquered much of Europe, Britain, Greece, and parts of North Africa and the Middle East. They spread their language and alphabet to many of these places.

Much Roman writing was carved on stone buildings and monuments. The alphabet used for stone carving was made up of the kinds of letters we call capitals.

But some writing was done with feather pens and ink on parchment, which is a kind of thick, stiff paper made of sheepskin. In time, the shapes of the capital letters were changed so that they were easier to make with a pen. This new writing was called cursive script.

About 1,200 years ago, some priests in what is now France began to make a Bible that was written entirely by hand on parchment pages. The priests wanted the book to be as beautiful as possible, so they changed the Roman cursive script letters into shapes they thought were more attractive. They also wanted to save time and space, so they used smaller letters. These little letters had been gradually developing since the time of the Greeks. They are the lower-case letters that we use today.

A French manuscript from the 800's contains both capital letters and the new "little," or lower-case, letters that had only recently begun to be used.

From Sounds to Letters 41

The story of w and u

Why do we call *w* "double *u*"? It's made out of two *v*'s—*vv*—so it's really a double *v*, not a double *u*.

Until the early A.D. 1000's, there was no *w* in the Old English alphabet. (Old English was the earliest version of the English language.) There was, however, a letter that looked somewhat like a *p* and was used for the sound *wuh*. In 1066, people called Normans who spoke Old French, a variety of the language that became modern French, conquered England. The Normans brought monks with them to do most of their writing. Of course, the writing was in Old French, but the monks often had to use Old English words. This was sometimes a problem because the Normans had no letter for the *wuh* sound.

42 Letters to Words

The monks solved the problem with their letter *v*, which they used for the vowel sounds *oo* and *uh*, as well as for the consonant sound *vee*. The *wuh* sounded like *oo-uh* to the monks, so they pushed two *v*'s together—*vv*—to make a new letter for the *oo-uh* sound. But because they wrote their *v* either as *v* or *u*, they often wrote the new letter with two *u*'s— *uu*. They called the letter "double v," but in English it became "double u."

Hundreds of years later, Italian printers began to use *v* only for the consonant sound *vee*, and *u* for the vowel sounds *oo* and *uh*. Thus, *u* came into the alphabet, making 25 letters. Only one more letter was needed to make the English alphabet the way it is today.

A dot and a tail

When the French monks made a lower-case *i*, it had no dot. It looked like a stubby *l*. When one of these *i*'s stood next to an *l*, it was easy to confuse the two letters for an *h*. And when two *i*'s were used side by side, as they often are in Latin, they could be mistaken for *n* or *u*. Sometime during the 1000's, someone solved this problem. The letter *i* began to appear in manuscripts with a dot over it. And we have been putting dots over our lower-case *i*'s ever since.

But there was still sometimes a problem when two *i*'s were used together. They might look like two *l*'s. To solve this problem, a tail was often added to the second *i*, like this—*ij*. Later, an *i* at the beginning of a word was also written with a tail.

In those days, the letter *i* stood for two sounds. One was the vowel sound *eye* that we give it now. The other was a consonant sound like *yuh*. But during the 1500's, Spanish printers began using *i* for the vowel sound and *j* for the consonant sound. English printers quickly borrowed this idea. They used *j* for the *juh* sound we give it now, and put it into the alphabet right after *i*. And that is why our alphabet now has 26 letters.

With those 26 letters, we speak to each other silently in hundreds of ways—through books, magazines, newspapers, signs, the Internet, and many other things. These letters have been turned into raised dots that people who cannot see can feel and into shapes that people who cannot hear can make with their fingers. Letters have also been turned into clicks, buzzes, flashes of light, and flags for sending messages. The alphabet is perhaps the greatest of all inventions!

From Sounds to Letters

Letters of the alphabet

Aa

an Angry aardvark Alarming an addled Alligator

Letters to Words

Bb

a **B**ashful **b**ear **B**ehind
a **b**are **B**lueberry **b**ush

From Sounds to Letters   47

Cc

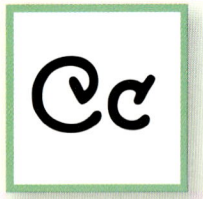

a Carefree chubby Cat in colorful Circus clothes

Dd

a **D**elighted **d**inosaur **D**evouring

a **d**elicious **D**inner

From Sounds to Letters

Ee

an Energetic elephant
Entertaining elegant Eels

50 Letters to Words

From Sounds to Letters **51**

Ff a Frightened fish Fleeing a Ferocious foe

52 Letters to Words

Gg   a **G**em-adorned **g**roup of
Gleefully **g**rinning **G**enies

Hh   **H**ungry **h**amsters **H**appily **h**auling
a **H**uge **h**am

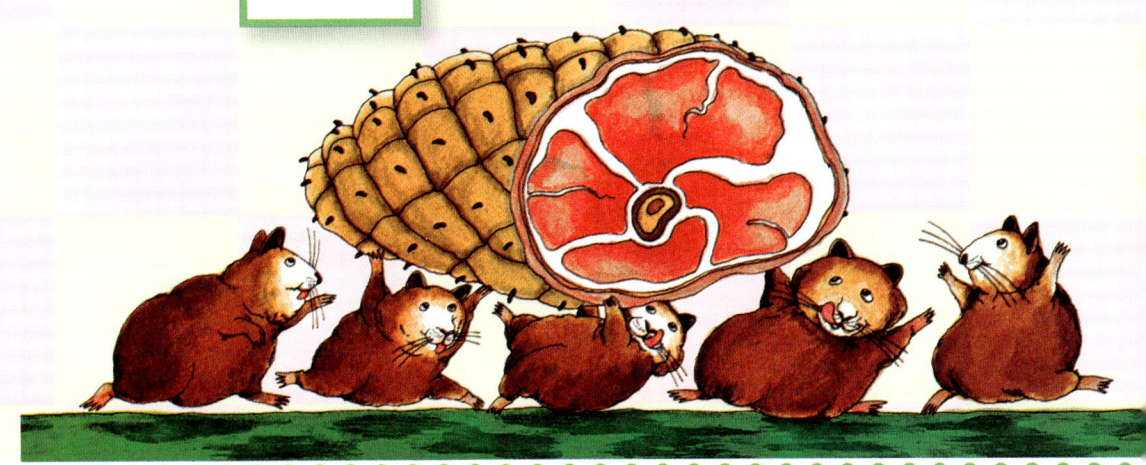

From Sounds to Letters

Ii

an **I**cy **i**mpresario **I**nstructing **i**mpudent **I**nsects

54 Letters to Words

Jj Jovial jabberwocks Jesting in a jumbled Jungle

From Sounds to Letters 55

Kk

a **K**indly **k**angaroo **K**nitting

a **k**nobby **K**eepsake

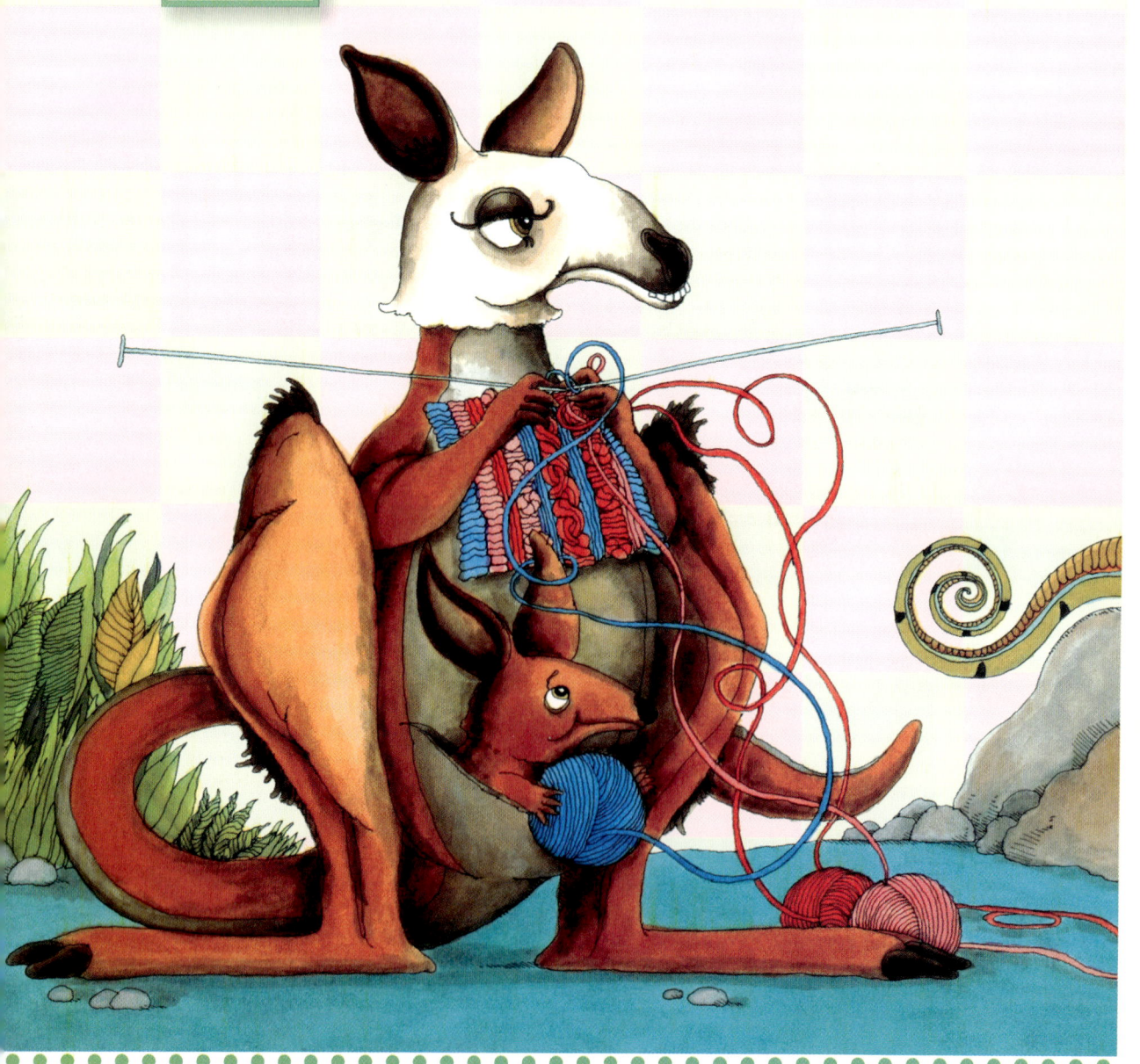

Ll

Lazy lizards Lying in a littered Lair

From Sounds to Letters

Mm

a Moody monster Moaning
on a misty Mountaintop

a Near-sighted nightingale Napping

in a neat Nest

Nn

58 Letters to Words

Oo

an **O**verstuffed **o**ctopus
Ogling **o**rnate **O**ysters

Pp

a **P**arty of **p**rim **P**igs
pompously **P**icknicking

From Sounds to Letters

Qq

a **Q**uarrelsome **q**ueen **Q**uashing a **q**uaking **Q**uintet

From Sounds to Letters 61

Rr

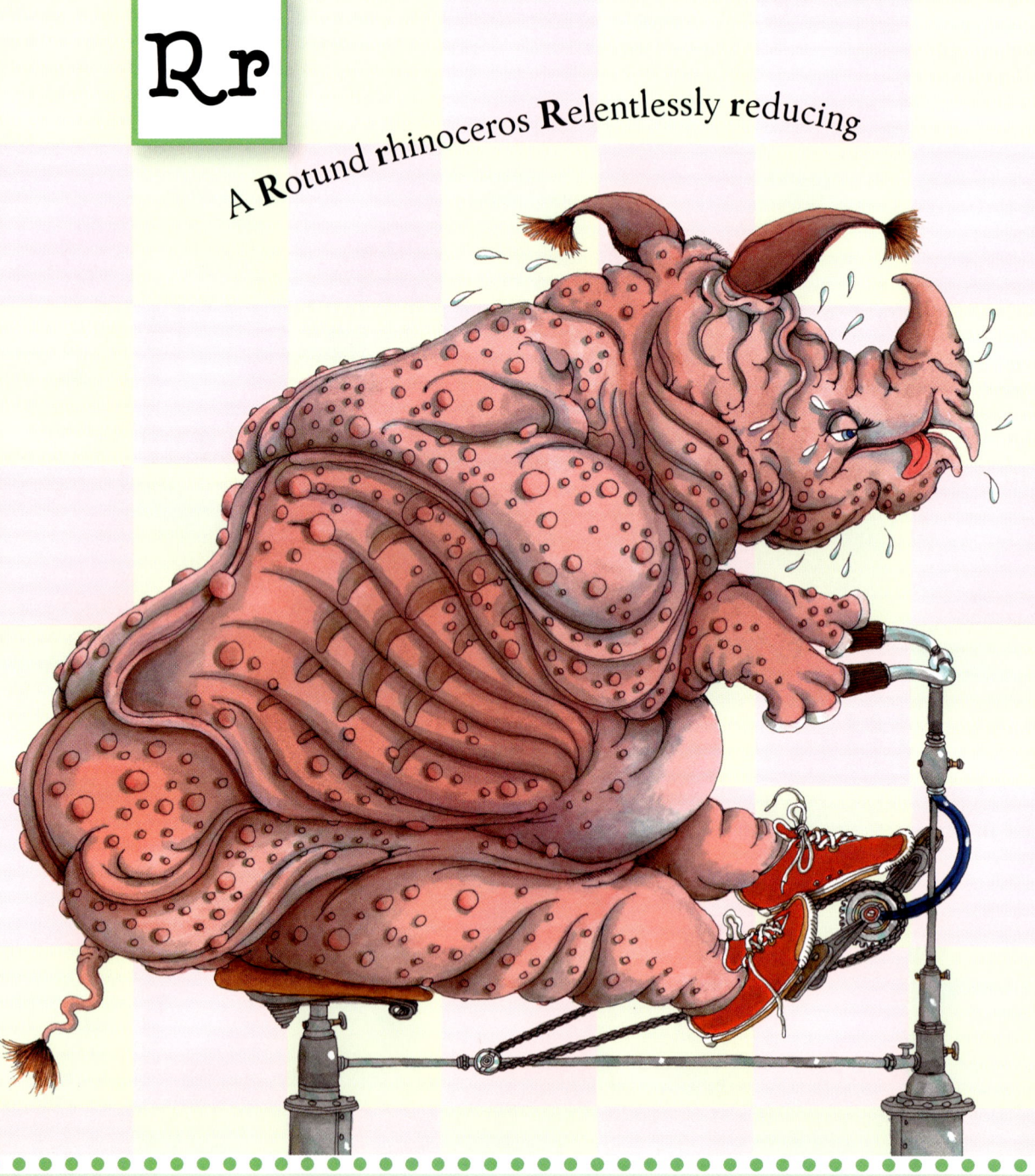

A **R**otund **r**hinoceros **R**elentlessly **r**educing

Letters to Words

a **S**tylish skunk **S**eated on a short **S**tump

Ss

a **T**idy **t**iger **T**imidly **t**aking a **T**edious **t**rip

Tt

From Sounds to Letters

Uu

an Unlucky uncle Under a useless Umbrella

Letters to Words

From Sounds to Letters 65

Vv

a Vain vampire
Viewing a vacant Vault

Ww

a Wealthy worm Wearing a weighty White wig

Xx

an eXuberant ox eXamining an extraordinary Xylophone

From Sounds to Letters

Yy

Yacking young Yaks in a yard of Yellow yams

68   Letters to Words

Zz

a Zealous zebra Zigzagging a Zany zeppelin

From Sounds to Letters

2,000 years of

Semite alphabet

Phoenician alphabet

ΑΒΓΔΕΖΗΘΙΚΛΜΝΞ

Greek alphabet

ABCDEFGHIJKLMNOP

Roman alphabet

70 Letters to Words

the alphabet

ΟΠΡΣΤΥΦΧΨΩ

QRSTUVWXYZ

From Sounds to Letters 71

Other alphabets

Almost all languages have an alphabet. But the alphabets of other languages are often very different from ours, just as the Phoenician, Greek, and Roman alphabets were all different. The Hebrew alphabet, for example, is written from right to left, so that the letter "aleph" appears last in the list below, even though it is first in alphabetical order.

abcoefghilmn

Gaelic alphabet

תשרקצץפףעסנמםלכיך

Hebrew alphabet

АБВГДЕЖЗИЙКЛМНОПР

Russian alphabet

O P R S T U

אבגדהוזחט

СТУФХЦЧШЩЪЫЬЭЮЯ

From Sounds to Letters

There's a Hippo in the Attic Eating a Sandwich

Most words are names of such things as animals, objects, or actions. But why do we call things by certain names? You know that a hippopotamus is a certain kind of animal—but why is it called a hippopotamus? You know what an attic is, and what a sandwich is. But how did they get these names? There's a wonderful story behind most words—and here are some of the stories.

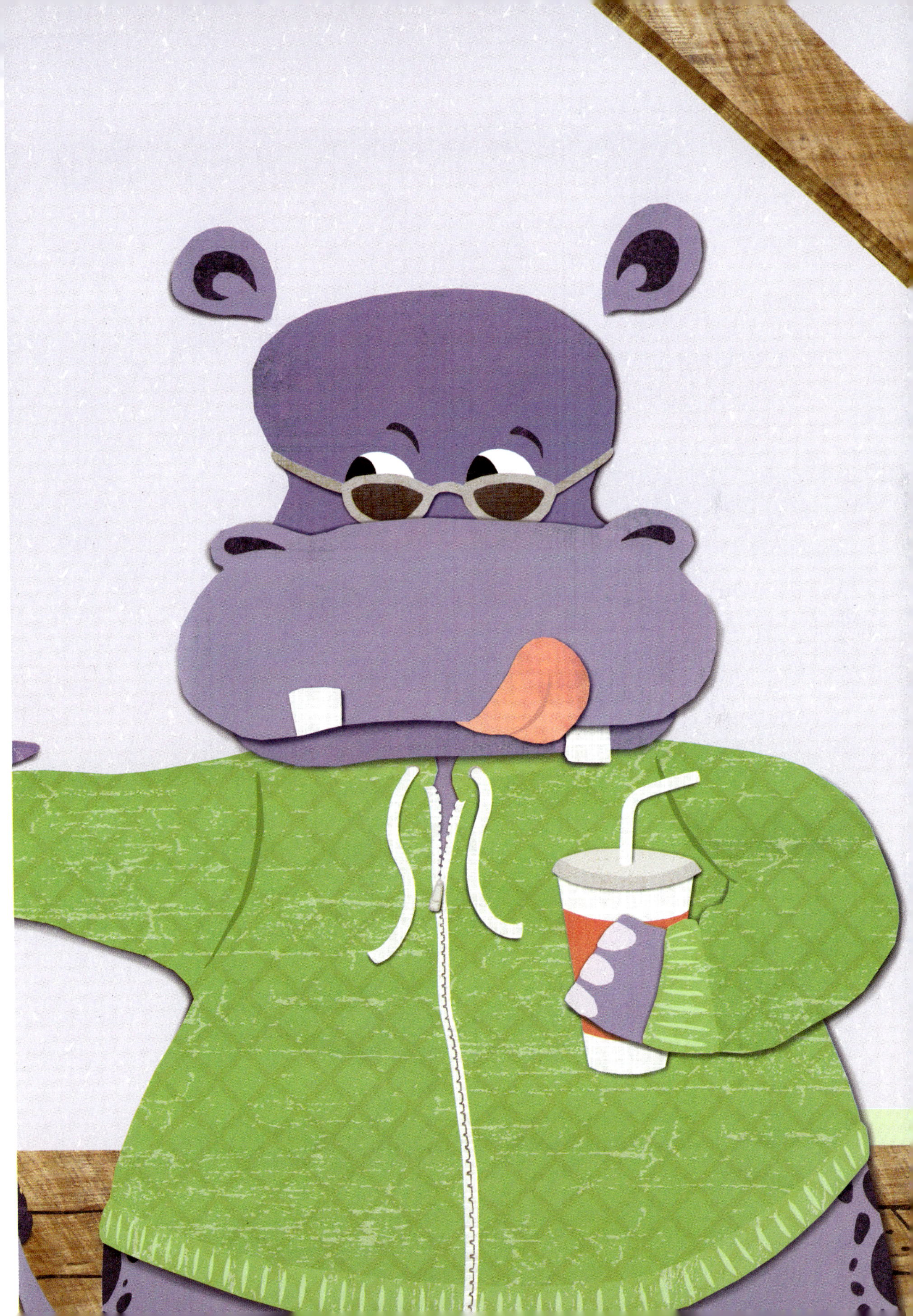

Menu meanings

Menu
Clam Chowder
Hamburger Sandwich
Coleslaw
French Fries
Chocolate Sundae

That looks like a pretty good lunch, doesn't it? But where did these rather strange names come from? Why do we call a lump of ground beef a *hamburger* or slices of meat between two pieces of bread a *sandwich*? What in the world does *coleslaw* mean? And why is a dish of ice cream with chocolate syrup called a sundae? Here's how each of the foods on this menu got its name.

Clam chowder is a soup made out of clams and vegetables. Soup is usually cooked in a big pot. And our word *chowder* comes from the French word *chaudière*, which means "pot."

Letters to Words

There is no ham at all in hamburger. It's made of ground beef. Americans think of hamburger as being an American food, but it really came from Germany. Long ago, many German people came to America to live. They brought with them recipes for their favorite foods. One of these foods was a kind of meatball made of ground beef. These meatballs were supposed to have been invented in the German city of Hamburg, so they became known as hamburgers.

And why should slices of meat between two pieces of bread be called a *sandwich?* The word *sandwich* comes from the name of an English nobleman. Long ago, there lived a nobleman with the title Earl of Sandwich. According to one story, the earl loved to play cards. One day, he was playing cards and didn't want to stop for dinner, even though he was hungry. So he told a servant to bring him some slices of meat between two pieces of toasted bread. Others tried this new way of eating bread and meat together. They called it a *sandwich* in honor of the earl. To this day, any kind of food that is served between slices of bread is called a sandwich.

Coleslaw is a spicy salad made of chopped cabbage. This salad comes from the Netherlands, and its name is made up of two Dutch words—*kool,* meaning "cabbage," and *sla,* meaning "salad." So coleslaw simply means "cabbage salad"—just what it is.

You might think that French fried potatoes got their name because they were first made in France. But that's not the reason. Cooks at restaurants and hotels often cut meat and vegetables into long strips. This process is called *Frenching*.

When American cooks first began to fry potatoes that had been Frenched, they called them Frenched fried potatoes. Now, we just call them French fries.

Do you like ketchup on your French fries? Lots of people do. It gives the French fries a tangy taste. Ketchup—or catchup, or catsup, as it is also spelled—is a tomato sauce. Its name comes from the Chinese word *ke-tsiap*, which was the name of a pickled fish sauce. Originally, there weren't even any tomatoes in ke-tsiap! Tomatoes were added in the 1700's, and the sauce became known as tomato ketchup. Eventually, the "tomato" part was dropped. Today, any sauce called "ketchup" always has tomatoes in it.

There are many stories about how the ice cream sundae got its name. One story comes from Manitowoc, Wisconsin. More than 100 years ago, sundaes were rather special. You could get them only in little stores called ice cream parlors, and you could usually get them only on a Sunday. They had no name then, so if you wanted one, you just asked for a dish of "special ice cream."

Letters to Words

A dish of the special ice cream, please.

sundae

One weekday, a little girl came into Mr. George Giffy's ice cream parlor in Manitowoc. She asked for a dish of the special ice cream. Mr. Giffy told her that he sold the special ice cream only on Sunday. "Then this must be Sunday," said the little girl, "because that's the kind of ice cream I want." That gave Mr. Giffy the idea to begin calling the special ice cream a "Sunday." And, somehow, it later got turned into "sundae." However it got its name, a sundae is still a treat!

There's a Hippo in the Attic

Splash dogs and

Did you ever hear of an animal called a river horse? Or a pebble worm? Or a splash dog? Probably not. But these are the meanings of the names of three animals you know very well. Most names are words that mean something. Sometimes, the things they mean are funny or surprising.

hippopotamus

crocodile

The hippopotamus was named by the ancient Greeks. The first Greeks who saw a hippopotamus snorting and splashing in a river must have thought it looked like a fat horse, because the word *hippopotamus* means "river horse" in Greek.

The ancient Greeks also gave the crocodile its name. The first crocodile they saw must have been lying with its feet tucked under it on a gravel beach, so that it looked like a legless worm. The Greeks put together their words for *pebble* and *worm* to make the word *krokodilos*, which means "pebble worm."

river horses

poodle

spider

Poodle comes from the German word *Pudelhund*. In German, *pudeln* means "to splash water," and *hund* means "dog." So a poodle is a "splash dog." Poodles were originally bred to retrieve such birds as ducks for hunters, so they spent a lot of time splashing through water.

Our name for the bug called a beetle comes from the Old English word *bitula*, which means "little biter." Spider also comes from an Old English word, *spithre*, which means "spinner."

duck

Duck is from the Old English word *duce*. Pronounced *dook uh*, it means "diving bird." This is a good name, because ducks dive down in the water to get their food.

There's a Hippo in the Attic

moose

octopus

The names of many North American animals come from Indian words. The word *moose* is almost like the Algonquin word *moos-u*, which means "he strips off bark." The Indians gave this big animal that name because when they are very hungry, moose eat bark that they strip off young trees.

The name *octopus* comes from two Greek words—*okto,* meaning "eight," and *pous,* meaning "foot." So *octopus* means "eight-footed," because this animal has eight wiggly tentacles.

One of the last kinds of animals to be named was the dinosaur. When dinosaur bones were first discovered, scientists used Greek and Latin words to make up names that would best describe these great reptiles. The word *dinosaur* itself was the first name they made up. It comes from the Greek words *deinos,* which means "terrible" and *sauros,* which means "lizard." Although scientists once thought that dinosaurs were "terrible lizards," they now know that they weren't related to lizards at all. And some of the dinosaurs weren't so terrible, either!

The first specific kind of dinosaur to be named was *Megalosaurus.* Scientists thought it was a giant lizard. They named it by combining the Greek words *megalou,* meaning "great," and *sauros.* So *Megalosaurus* simply means "great lizard."

Wind-eyes in the posts

It's spring-cleaning time at your house. You're going to wash the wind-eyes in the elegant room. Then you're going to help your mother paint the posts in the cooking place.

That sounds strange, doesn't it? But, as a matter of fact, every house really does have lots of "wind-eyes," "posts" in every room, a "cooking place," and, usually, an "elegant room," too. It also has "pieces" in the windows and "splits" on its "cover"!

What are wind-eyes? Well, long ago, Vikings living in England (now part of the United Kingdom) had openings in the walls of their houses to let in light and air. To the Vikings, the openings seemed like eyes looking out at the wind. So they called them "wind-eyes." Their word for "wind-eye" was *vindauga*—and that's where our word *window* comes from. So *window* really means "wind-eye."

There's a Hippo in the Attic

And what about the glass in a window—the panes? How did they get this name? At one time, people used pieces of cloth to cover the window openings in walls. Long ago, in England, such a piece of cloth was called a *pannus,* from a Latin word meaning "a piece of cloth." Later, that word was changed to *pan,* and then *pane,* and simply meant "piece." Thus, a windowpane is a window "piece."

The "posts" in every room in a house are the walls. Long ago, when a Roman army made camp, the soldiers put walls around the camp's four sides. The walls were made of wooden posts pounded into the ground. The Roman word for *post* was *vallus,* and the wall of posts was called a *vallum.* So, our word *wall,* which comes from *vallum,* means "a row of posts."

We could call the attic of a house the "elegant room." This seems a strange name for a room that's usually full of junk. But here's how it works out.

Many people in England once thought the ancient Greek city of Athens must have been the most elegant and beautiful place in the world. They changed the Greek word *Attikos,* which means "of Athens" to *Attic,* and used it to mean something that was truly elegant. They built houses with rows of pillars along the top, as the Greeks had done. These pillars were said to be "Attic style." After a while, people called the whole top part of such a house an *attic.* So, the word *attic,* our name for the dusty, junk-filled room at the top of a house, really means something fine and elegant, like ancient Athens.

The part of a house where cooking is done is the kitchen. Why not just call this room the "cooking room"? How did it get the odd name *kitchen?*

The word *kitchen* comes from the Latin word *coquina,* which means "cooking." Roman soldiers took that word into England, where it became *cychene* and meant a place where cooking was done. *Cychene* became *kuchene,* and finally *kitchen.* So kitchen really means "a cooking place."

And, last of all, every house has a cover with splits on it. Our word *roof* comes from the Old English word *hrof,* meaning "cover." Roofs have shingles, and shingles used to be made of pieces of wood that had been split. The Latin word *scindula* means "split." In English, this word was changed to *shindle* and then to *shingle.* So a house with a shingle roof has a "cover" with "splits."

And that's the story of the wind-eyes, posts, elegant room, cooking place, cover, and splits of your house.

There's a Hippo in the Attic   85

A break, a lump,

Have you ever broken a fast? Yes, you have, lots of times. And you were never blamed for breaking it! Fast doesn't only mean "quick"; it also means to go without eating. You fast all night long, while you're asleep. Then, when you wake up in the morning and eat, you break your fast—that is, you stop fasting. And that's why we call our morning meal *breakfast*.

At noontime you eat a lump! The word *lunch* first meant a lump (or hunk) of bread or cheese. Another old word, *nuncheon*, meant a noontime drink. Word experts think *nuncheon* was changed to *luncheon*, meaning a lump of food at noontime.

Letters to Words

and a sip

Evening is suppertime. Supper is usually your biggest meal, so you'd be surprised if your mother gave you only soup and told you to "sip it." But that's what supper really means. It comes from the older word *sup*, which meant to sip a liquid. Nowadays, people usually say, "Let's have supper." Long ago, they were more likely to say, "Let us sup."

Do you use the word "dinner" instead of "supper"? *Dinner* originally meant the first meal of the day. It came from the Latin words *dis*, meaning "undo" or "break," and *jejunare*, meaning "to fast." So at dinner, you broke your fast. Later, the word was used for the midday meal, which was the main meal of the day. Finally, the fashionable classes began to take their main meal later in the day, and "dinner" became an evening meal.

There's a Hippo in the Attic

Wear words

*P*ants is a funny-sounding word. Where did such a word come from?

A long time ago, many plays had a character called Pantalone. And Pantalone usually wore long, red tights. The first kind of long trousers that men wore were quite tight-fitting, so they became known as pantaloons, after Pantalone's long tights. But because *pantaloons* is such a long word, it was soon shortened to *pants.* And that's what it has been ever since.

Lots of people wear pants made out of strong cotton cloth, usually dyed blue. Over the more than 100 years since they've been around, these pants have been called jeans, denims, dungarees, or Levi's. How did they get all these strange names?

Jeans comes from the name *Genes,* which is the French name for the city of Genoa, Italy, where a lot of cotton cloth

Letters to Words

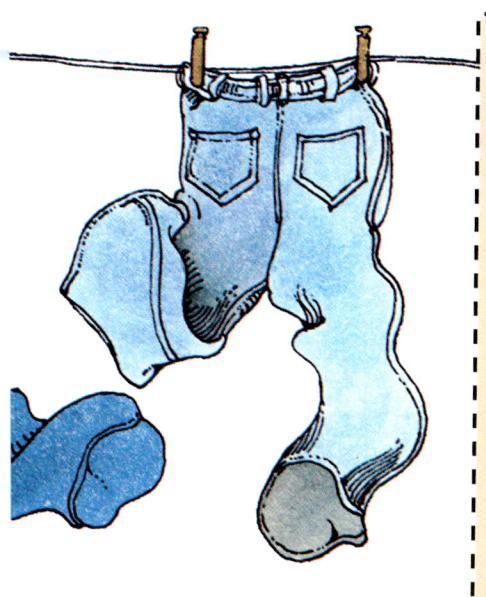

Fashion designers began making tight-fitting jeans out of the kind of knit fabric used to make leggings (far left and far right, above). They made up a new name for them, too—jeggings!

was made. French people called the cloth by their name for the city. We use the French name as our word for the pants.

Another kind of strong cotton cloth was made in the city of Nimes, France. The cloth was called serge de Nimes. And, of course, *denims* comes from *de Nimes*.

Dungarees comes from the East Indian word *dungri*. Long ago, English traders brought coarse cotton cloth called *dungri* back from India. In time, the English people changed the word to *dungaree*.

Levi's are named after a man, Levi Strauss. He was a clothing merchant who put metal fasteners on the pockets of pants to keep them from tearing.

We've made up a pretty funny modern word based on these kinds of pants, too—*jeggings. Jeggings* are leggings (tight-fitting, usually knit, pants) that are made to look like jeans. They sound kind of like the pantaloons of olden days, don't they?

There's a Hippo in the Attic   89

School words

Believe it or not, *school* means "spare time"!

The ancient Greeks believed that education was one of the most important things in life. Young Greeks would even use their spare time for learning. They liked to listen to those who were wise talk about science and other things. The Greek word *schole* means "spare time." A group of young Greeks who listened to teachers in their spare time was called a *schole*. And, of course, that's where our word *school* comes from.

Your schoolbooks owe their name to a tree. People in England once wrote on the thin, inner bark of beech trees. In Old English, the name of the beech tree was *boc*. After a while, *boc*, then *bok*, and finally *book* came to mean the writing on a sheet of bark. Now it means many sheets of paper, with writing or printing on them, all bound together.

The pen that you do your schoolwork with is named after a feather. For hundreds of years, people wrote with feathers. They cut the quills to a point and dipped them in ink. The Latin word for feather is *penna,* and so the feathers used for writing became known as *pens.* To this day, we still call any writing tool that uses ink a *pen.*

The word *pencil* comes from a Latin word, too. The word is *penicillus,* and means "brush" or "little tail." Artists used to call their smallest, pointed brushes pencils, because the brush looked like a little pointed tail. In time, the name came to be used for the pointed writing tool we call a pencil.

And why are schoolchildren sometimes called *pupils?* The Latin word *pupillae* means "little dolls." Long ago, that word came to mean children who were in the care of a teacher. It is from this word that we got the English word *pupil.*

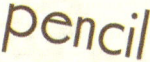

Bearders and tellers

It's easy to understand what the names of some jobs mean. A *lawyer* practices law. A *teacher* teaches. A *baker* bakes.

But many job names don't seem to have anything to do with the job itself. Why is a person who gives haircuts called a barber? And why is a person who works in a store called a clerk?

Barbers not only give haircuts, they also shave men. And that's how they got their name. The Latin word for beard was *barba,* so a man who shaves and trims beards is a barber, meaning "a bearder."

Long ago, in Europe, a priest or monk was called a cleric. That's a Latin word that means "priest." Priests, or clerics, were once just about the only people who knew how to read, write, and do arithmetic. So, they kept all the written records for kings and nobles. They figured out how much people owed in taxes, kept records of payments, and so on.

Hundreds of years later, when many people other than priests could read and write, anyone who kept written records, or worked with figures (numbers), was called a cleric. Later, this was shortened to clerk. People who work in stores and offices do a lot of writing and figuring, so they became known as clerks. If you know people who are clerks, they'll be surprised when you tell them that the name of their job really means "priest."

clerk

You might think that someone who is called a teller would tell things to people. But tellers work in banks. They count out money. The word *teller* really means "counter."

teller

There's a Hippo in the Attic   **93**

Why do we call the people who deliver letters and packages *mail carriers* when they're really carrying letters? It's because hundreds of years ago, in France, the first letter carriers had leather bags called *males* to carry letters in. When the people of England started having men deliver letters, the name of the bag was borrowed from the French. But the spelling became *mail* instead of *male*. So *mail* really means "a leather bag," and a mail carrier is a "bag carrier."

mail carrier

Today, an engineer is a person who plans and builds roads, dams, bridges, buildings, airplanes, ships, and many other things. But long ago, an engineer was part of an army. In those days, armies often had to capture cities and castles. But the cities and castles had high walls, so the armies had to try to

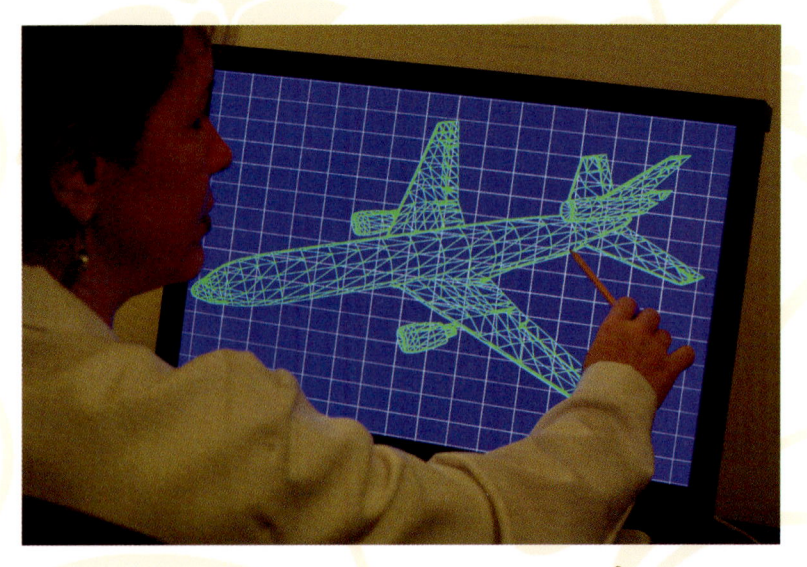

engineer

94 Letters to Words

knock down the walls or get over them. To do this, they used machines. They had tall wooden towers to get men over the walls, battering rams to pound the walls until they fell down, and catapults that hurled huge rocks at the walls. These machines were called war engines. The word *engine* meant both "skill" and "invention." The men who built the machines were called *engineers,* meaning "skilled inventors." And that's what we still call people who plan and build things.

grocer

A person who owns or works in a grocery store is called a grocer. The word *grocer* comes from the word *gross,* which means "a large amount." Hundreds of years ago, there were no food stores, just stores where you could buy spices. The people who owned such stores were called *spicers en gross,* which meant "spice sellers in large amounts." But people shortened this to *grosser,* and spelled it *grocer.* So when people started to sell large amounts of all kinds of food, they were called grocers, and their stores became known as grocery stores.

Nice villains

Can a villain be nice? Can a chair be naughty?

Long ago, they could. Many of the words we use once had different meanings. *Nice, villain,* and *naughty* all meant something quite different from what they do now.

Nice once meant "foolish." It comes from the Latin word *nescius,* which means "not knowing." A nice person was once someone who didn't know anything!

Today, a villain is a bad person. But the word *villain* once simply meant "farmhand." In Latin, a *villa* was a big farmhouse, owned by a rich man or noble. A *villanus* was a man who worked the farmlands that belonged to the *villa.* The word *villanus* got changed to *villein* in French, and then to *villain* in English. Because the villains had poor manners and no education, the nobles looked down on them, as if they were bad people. So, slowly, the word *villain* came to mean someone who was wicked.

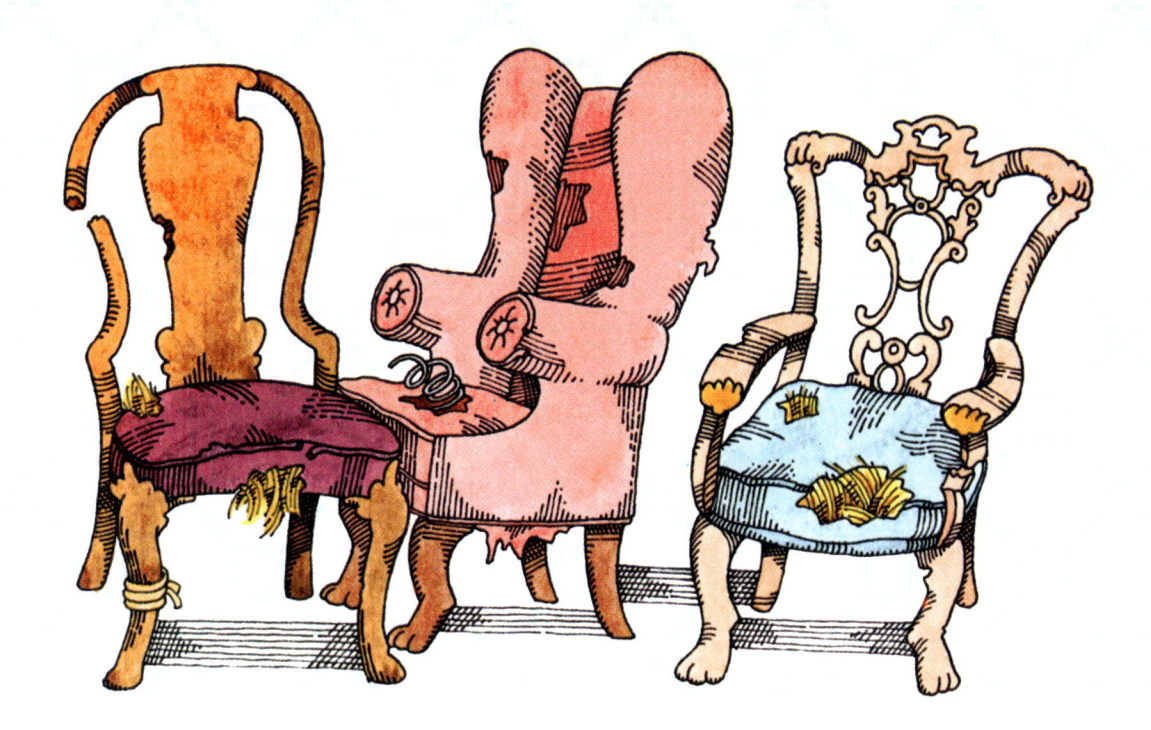

and naughty chairs

Long ago, someone might have said that a chair was naughty. A naughty chair would have been a chair that wasn't much good. *Naughty* meant "good for nothing." It comes from the word *naught*, which we still use to mean "nothing."

Quick used to mean "alive" instead of "fast," as it does now. It comes from the Old English word *cwic*. When people said someone was quick, they meant the person was alive. When they wanted someone to do something in a hurry, they said, "be quick," meaning "be alive, move fast, like a live person." After a while, *quick* came to mean "fast," as it does now.

And if someone calls you "silly," you shouldn't care. *Silly*, which comes from the Middle English word *seely*, used to mean "happy."

Howls, thumps, and creaks

It was midnight, and the sky was black and stormy. The wind *howled*, and there were *crashes* of thunder. Rain *pattered* sharply on the roof of the old, haunted house. A shutter, swinging in the wind, went *bang-bang, bang-bang* against the side of the house.

"I'm not afraid," the boy who had gone into the house on a dare said to himself.

But suddenly, he heard another noise. From down in the cellar, there came the long, slow *creak* of a door opening. The boy's hair stood on end as he heard the *clank* of dragging chains. Then— *thump ... thump ... thump*. Something was coming up the stairs! With a *shriek*, the boy rushed out of the house.

One reason why ghost stories are so much fun is that they use words that help us imagine the spooky sounds of a haunted house at night. Words such as *howl, crash, patter, bang, creak, clank, thump,* and *shriek* are really imitations of sounds.

Our language is full of words that imitate sounds. *Thud* is a word that imitates the sound something heavy makes when it falls to the ground. *Squish* sounds like the noise your feet make when you walk through mud. *Squawk, bark, croak, purr, buzz,* and *grunt* sound like noises certain animals make. How many other noise-words can you think of?

Letters to Words

There's a Hippo in the Attic

Cut-off words

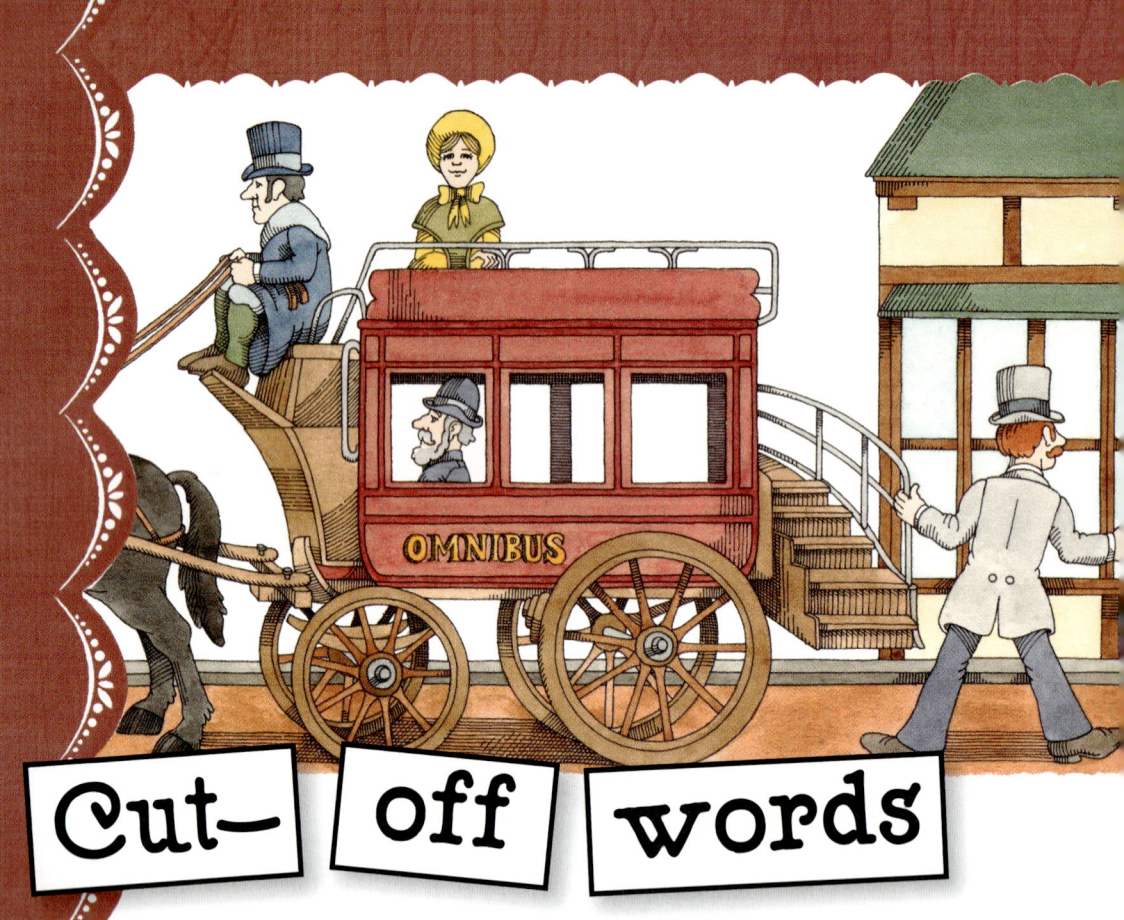

Sometimes, we don't like to take the time to say long words. So we shorten the words by using only part of them. Our language is full of such parts of words, or "cut-off words."

Bus is one of these cut-off words. It comes from the word *omnibus*. Most people once had to walk to get anywhere they wanted to go. Only wealthy people, who could afford to own horses or carriages, were able to get about quickly and easily. But in the early 1800's in France, big carriages were used to make it easier for everyone to get about in the city of Paris. These carriages traveled back and forth on regular routes along many of the city's streets, picking up people who wanted to go somewhere. It cost very little to ride on one of these carriages, so almost everyone could afford it.

bus

Because these carriages were for everyone, they were called omnibuses, from a Latin word that means "for all." Soon, omnibuses appeared in English cities, too. There, people quickly shortened the name to *bus*.

Cab is short for the French word *cabriolet*, which comes from a word meaning "to leap or caper." A cabriolet was a light, two-wheeled carriage that bounced a lot, so the name was a good one.

cab

There's a Hippo in the Attic   **101**

Gun is another cut-off word the English language adopted from the French. *Gun* is really part of the word *dragon*. The first guns were called dragons because they shot out smoke and fire, the way dragons were thought to do.

Are you a baseball or football fan? This kind of fan comes from the word *fanatic*. A fanatic is someone who gets wildly excited about something he or she believes in.

Mathematics, examination, cellular telephone, electronic mail and *World Wide Web camera* are all words that we often shorten—such as saying *e-mail* for *electronic mail*. What "cut-off words" have we made from the others?

Letters to Words

Invented words

Suppose you invented a wonderful new kind of shoe—one that allowed you to run so fast that you would win every race! What would you name such a great invention?

You could name it the Velocidrome! The word *veloci* means "fast" in the Greek language and the word *dromeus* means "runner," so *velocidrome* would mean "fast runner."

Lots of inventions are named this way—by putting together two or three words to make a brand new word that tells what the invention does. That's how the telephone, photograph, and biofuel got their names.

We use a telephone to send the sound of our voice to someone who is far away. And *telephone* means "far sound." It's a word that is made up from two Greek words—*tele*, which means "far," and *phone*, which means "sound."

If *telephone* means "far sound," can you guess what *television* means? That's right—it means "far sight." And how about *telemedicine*? Doctors who practice telemedicine can diagnose and treat patients who are far away by using telecommunications technology.

telephone

photograph

A photograph is a picture that's made by letting light touch a piece of film or, in a digital camera, a sensor. *Photograph* is made up from the Greek words *photos*, meaning "light," and *graphein*, which means "to draw" or "write." Thus, *photograph* means "to draw with light."

From the time they were invented, most automobiles have run on gasoline. Gasoline is a fossil fuel, a substance that is made from once-living material that has been dead for millions of years. But beginning in the late 1900's, many car manufacturers began to make cars that can run on a different kind of fuel. That fuel—called ethanol—is made from living crops that can be re-grown every year. Ethanol, and other fuels like it, are called biofuels. The word *biofuel* was made up from the Greek word *bios*, meaning "life," and an Old French word, *feuaile*, which came from a Latin word for fire. So biofuel is a living substance that burns.

biofuel

Letters to Words

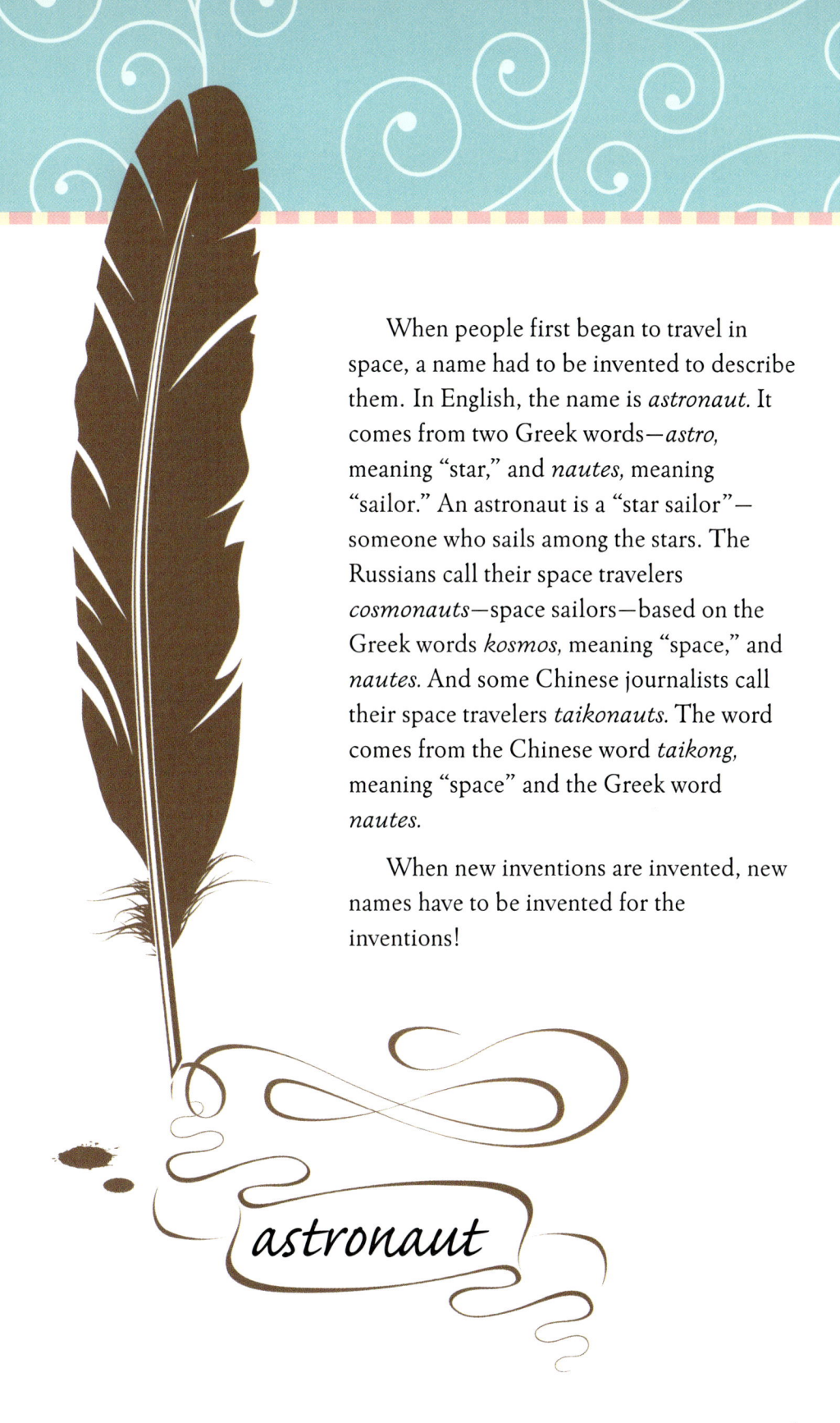

When people first began to travel in space, a name had to be invented to describe them. In English, the name is *astronaut*. It comes from two Greek words—*astro*, meaning "star," and *nautes*, meaning "sailor." An astronaut is a "star sailor"—someone who sails among the stars. The Russians call their space travelers *cosmonauts*—space sailors—based on the Greek words *kosmos*, meaning "space," and *nautes*. And some Chinese journalists call their space travelers *taikonauts*. The word comes from the Chinese word *taikong*, meaning "space" and the Greek word *nautes*.

When new inventions are invented, new names have to be invented for the inventions!

astronaut

What's in a Name?

Do you know that both your first and last name are words that have special meanings? They are. On the next few pages you will find many first and last names and what they mean. Perhaps you will find your names, or the names of some of your friends. And you may be surprised to learn what some of the names mean!

LIONS

#	NAME	POINTS
15	ALEXA	2
4	CARLOS	1
8	EVANGELINA	
7	SKYLAR	1
12	LOGAN	
3	RYAN	
9	ELENA	
17	KATRINA	
2	SAMMY	
11	EVAN	
21	NI	
1		

What does your

Deborah

Gavin

Thomas

Kwame

Tanisha

Are you a bee? That's what you are if your name is Deborah—because that's what Deborah means! Are you a white falcon? You are if your name is Gavin! Even if you don't have any brothers or sisters, you're really a twin—if your name is Thomas! If you were born on a Saturday and you are a boy, you're a Kwame. And if you are a girl who was born on a Monday, you are a Tanisha.

108   Letters to Words

first name mean?

Almost everyone's first name is a word that means something. Many of these word-names are thousands of years old. They come from many different languages. Here are some names and what they mean.

Albert, Alberta, Alberto, Alina, Bert, Claire, Clara, Elaine, Ellen, Elena, Helen, Helena, Kiyoshi, Myung, and Quon mean *bright* or *brightness*. Robert, Roberta, and Roberto mean *bright fame*.

Catherine, Inessa, Kaisa, Kaitlyn, Kara, Karen, Katherine, Kathleen, Kathryn, Katie, Pavit, Pumeet, and Sook mean *pure*.

Elisa, Elizabeth, Isabel, Isabella, and Lisa mean *God's promise* or *belongs to God*. Makayla, Mia, Michael, Michaela, Michelle, Miguel, and Mikhail mean *who is like God*.

Liliana, Lillian, Lily, Lis, Susan, Susannah, Suzanne, and Zsa Zsa mean *lily*. Other girls' names come from the names of flowers, too: Dahlia, Daisy, Heather, Jasmine, Rose, Violet, Yasmin, and Zinnia.

Roberto *Lisa*
Michael
Ellen
Yasmin
Bert

What's in a Name?   **109**

Abubakar, Adelaide, Alicia, Allison, Arthur, Brianna, Brian, Earl, Kareem, Nabil, Patricia, Patrick, and Saree mean *noble*.

Greta, Gretchen, Lulu, Maggie, Margaret, Meg, Megan, and Peggy mean *pearl*.

Aisha, Ava, Chaim, Eva, Eve, Evangelina, and Zoe mean *life*.

Alain, Alan, Beau, Bonnie, Bonny, Farah, Hassan, Hussein, Jamal, Jamila, Kane, Kenneth, Lalit, Linda, Nani, and Shaquille mean *beautiful* or *handsome*.

Boris, Chad, Drew, Guy, Lois, Louis, Louise, Luis, Luisa, and Kelly mean *great warrior*.

Andrea, Andrei, Andrew, Carla, Carlos, Carol, Charles, Ethan, Kang-Dae, Karl, Tut, Valentina, Valerie, Valeria, and Zuberi mean *strong*.

Noah, Salama, Salim, Serena, and Yani mean *peaceful*.

Evan, Ian, Ivan, Jack, Jan, Janaya, Janis, Joanna, Johanna, John, Juan, Juanita, Sean, Shawn, and Sheena mean *God is gracious*.

Brian
Greta
Shaquille
Kang-Dae
Valerie
Evan
Johanna

Sophia
Hannah
Jada

110   Letters to Words

Adriana, Blake, Cole, Darcy, Donovan, Dwayne, Ebony, Keara, Leila, Nigel, Khrishna, and Melanie mean *black* or *dark*.

Derek, Donald, Eric, Erica, Ricardo, Richard, Saddam, Vasili, and Vladimir mean *ruler*. Narendra, Rex, Roy, and Ryan mean *king*. Darice, Dionne, Malika, and Riona mean *queen*. Amira, Sadie, Sara, and Sarah mean *princess*. Amir, Brendan, and Kumar mean *prince*.

Ann, Anna, Anne, Annie, Hannah, and Janina mean *grace*.

Asia, Chelsea, Cheyenne, Dakota, Eden, Georgia, Isla, Logan, Paris, Savannah, Sierra, and Skye come from the names of places or geographic features around the world.

Alec, Alejandro, Alexa, Alexander, Alexandra, Alexis, Cassandra, Cassie, Sandra, and Sandy mean *defender of man or mankind*.

Dora, Dorothy, Matthew, Nathan, Ted, and Theodore mean *a gift of God*.

Dylan, Marina, Marisa, and Meryl mean *the sea*.

Alfred, Alfredo, Alfreda, Conan, Connor, Jada, Rashad, Sofia, or Sophia mean *wise* or *wise advisor*.

Dylan
Nigel *Alec*

What's in a Name? **111**

How last names were invented

Once upon a time, four men lived on the same street in a little town. They all had the same name—Tom. And that was the only name any of them had. In those days, only kings and nobles had last names. Most men and women had only first names.

Because the men had the same name, you might think people would get them mixed up. But there was a way of telling them apart. One Tom had a father named John, so he was called *Tom, John's son.* Another Tom, a baker, was

Tom, John's son

Tom the baker

112 Letters to Words

called *Tom the Baker*. The third Tom had red hair. He was known as *Tom the Red*. And the fourth Tom lived next to a park called the village green, so he was known to everyone as *Tom of the Green*.

Tom the Baker married a girl named Meg. She became known as *Meg, Tom the Baker's wife*. They had a little boy named John, and he was known as *John, the Baker's son*. But after a while, people got tired of saying all those words. So they simply called Tom the Baker, *Tom Baker*. His wife became *Meg Baker*, and his son was *John Baker*.

That's how many last names came to be. You will see more examples of how people got their last names on the pages that follow.

Tom the white

Tom of the green

What's in a Name?

Last names from first names

Before there were last names, children were often known by their father's name. If a man named Robert has a boy named John, the boy might be known as *John, Robert's*—meaning that he was Robert's son. If Robert had a daughter named Poll, she might be called *Poll, Robert's*. After a while, these became regular last names. When a boy grew up and married, his wife and children would take his last name. So, if your name ends with *s*, as in Richards, Roberts, Thomas, Adams, or Rogers, it came from someone who, long ago, had a father named Richard, Robert, Thomas, Adam, or Roger.

When people began to write last names, they often turned an *'s* ending of a name into *es*, *is*, or *ez*. Thus, names such as Jones and Hughes mean *John's* and *Hugh's*. Names such as Davis, Harris, and Willis mean *Davey's*, *Harry's*, and *Wil's*. And Rodriguez and Hernandez mean *Rodrigo's* and *Hernando's*.

Boys were often called by their father's name with the word "son" added. If Wil had a son called Jack, the boy might be known as *Jack, Wil's son*. These kinds of names became regular last names, too. So if your last name ends in *son* or *sen*, as in *Wilson, Johnson, Gibson, Andersen,* or *Nelsen*, you got it from someone whose father was named *Wil, John, Gilbert, Anders,* or *Nels*.

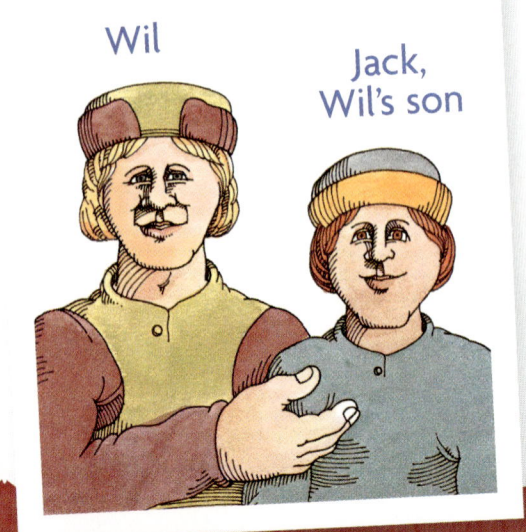

Wil

Jack, Wil's son

Letters to Words

People who spoke other languages added "son" to their fathers' names, too. If your name ends in *sohn, wicz, escu, vich,* or *ak,* those endings all mean "son."

People in some countries put their word for "son" in front of their fathers' names. *Mac, Mc,* and *Fitz* all mean "son of." And the prefix *O* before a name—such as in O'Hara or O'Reilly—means "grandson of" or "descendant of."

In some countries, a child traditionally took part of the last names of both the mother and the father. For example, Julio, the son of Rodrigo Ruiz y Gonzalez and Maria Lopez y Chavez, would have been known as *Julio Ruiz y Lopez* or *Julio Ruiz-Lopez.*

Others took religious names. *Katz* is short for "kohen tzedek," which is Hebrew for *priest of righteousness.*

In many American Indian tribes, a child has one name at birth and other names later in life. As a person takes a new name, he or she discards the earlier one. For example, a child may be given the birth name Sunrise Beauty; later, the family name Smooth Water; and then the adult name White Mountain.

Jack, Wil's son, and the Wilson family

What's in a Name?   115

Iron pounders and clothes makers

Lots of last names come from the kind of work people did.

For hundreds of years, one of the most important jobs was making things out of metal—tools, weapons, horseshoes, and so on. To make these things, metalworkers heated the metal until it was soft and then hammered it into shape. In an early version of the English language called Old English, a person who hammered metal was called a *smith*.

Metalworkers in other countries were usually also called by a name that meant "to hammer metal." When people began to take last names, many metalworkers took the name of their job. So if your name is Smith, Schmidt, Herrera, Ferris, Ferraro, Kowalski, Kovacs, or MacGowan, you probably had an ancestor who was a metalworker.

Letters to Words

TAYLOR

The word *mill* means "grind," and people who ground flour were called *millers.* That's where the names Miller, Milner, Mueller, and Molinaro come from.

People who make clothes are tailors. The names Taylor, Snider, Schneider, and Sarto all mean "tailor."

People once drove carts and wagons for a living, just as they drive trucks today. If your name is Carter, Porter, Wagner, or Schroeder, you probably got the name from someone who drove a cart or wagon.

Is your name Baker, Baxter, Fournier, Piekarz, or Boulanger? If so, you may have had an ancestor who was a baker.

Are you a Zimmerman? Then one of your ancestors may have been a carpenter.

What's in a Name?

Redheads and curly

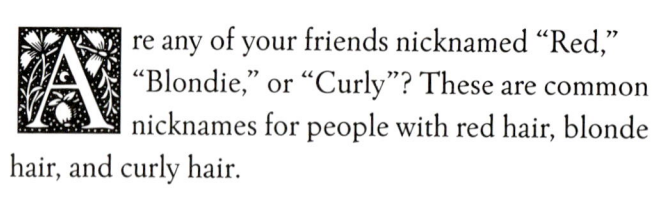

Are any of your friends nicknamed "Red," "Blondie," or "Curly"? These are common nicknames for people with red hair, blonde hair, and curly hair.

Hundreds of years ago, many people took such nicknames for their last names. A man might call himself "Will the Red" or "Tom Curly." If your last name is Flynn, Kilroy, Reed, Reid, Read, Rossi, Roth, Russell, or Zhu, your name means "red." If you are a White, Wise, Weiss, Whitehead, Whitlock, Whitman, Blanchard, Blount, or Bannon, your name may come from someone with light hair. And if you are a Krause, Kruse, Cassidy, or Rizzo, you probably had an ancestor who was a "Curly."

tops

Many other nicknames also became last names. Names such as Long, Laing, Hoch, and Longfellow were nicknames for tall people. Gao, Kao, Littell, Short, Small, Bass, Basset, Kline, Klein, Kurtz, Block, Malec, and Grubb were nicknames for people who were short. If your last name is Blythe, Corliss, Murray, Froh, Merriman, Blaha, Felicitas, Masoud, or Allegretti, you got your name from a good-natured person, for these names all mean "happy" or "cheerful."

In long-ago times, when last names were first used, most people seldom left the little towns where they were born. Everyone in a town knew everyone else. If a new person came to town to live, the people called him "new man," or "newcomer." After a while, he might take that for his last name. That's what Newman, Newcomb, Doyle, Doran, and Gill mean.

Hills, brooks, woods,

Many last names come from places where people lived. A man named Robert who lived on a hill might call himself "Robert o' the Hill." A woman whose house was beside a brook might be known as "Nell of the Brook." After a while, these names were shortened to Robert Hill and Nell Brook.

Berg, Hill, Hull, Hilton, Downs, Downing, Lowe, Law, Knapp, Knowles, Peck, Barrows, Bryant, Maki, Dumont, Depew, Zola, and Jurek are all names that come from people who lived on top of, on the side of, or at the bottom of a hill.

Brooks, Burns, Beck, Rivera, and Arroyo are names that come from people who lived beside a stream.

120 Letters to Words

and towns

Wood, Woods, Atwood, Grove, Haywood, Boyce, DuBois, Foster, Forster, Holt, Hurst, Lim, Shaw, and Silva are names that come from people who lived near or worked in small forests.

Marsh, Morse, Moore, Mosher, Carr, Carson, Fenton, Kerr, Slaughter, and Tanaka are names that come from people who lived near a marsh, or swampy place.

Castle, Castillo, Castro, Zamecki, Burke, Burkhardt, Borg, Burris, and Burr lived near a castle. Longstreet, Lane, Strass, and Estrada lived near a road.

Lake, Loch, Lynn, Mears, Poole, and Pollard are all names that come from people who lived near lakes, ponds, or pools.

And Garfield, Meadows, Mead, Fields, Lee, Pratt, Tian, Van Camp, Vega, Murawski, and Campos are names that were given to people who lived near grassy fields.

People also have taken their last name from the town or region in which they were born or that they came from. Such names as Chen, Middleton, Kronenberg, London, and Modena all represent such places. Other people chose pleasant combinations of various words— such as *gold, silver, rose (rosen), mountain (berg), stone (stein),* and *valley (thal)*—to form such names as Goldberg, Silverstein, and Rosenthal.

What's in a Name?

Animals and birds

Some last names are the names of animals. This came about in one of several ways.

Hundreds of years ago, most signs had no writing on them, just a picture. Many of the signs in front of inns had a picture of an animal—a wolf, a bear, a lion, or some kind of bird. People who worked at inns, or lived near them, often took the name of the animal on the inn sign as their last name.

Other last names that are the names of animals come from nicknames. A man who was said to be "as smart as a fox" might have become known as Fox. And a very brave man might have been called Lion.

So, if your last name is the name of an animal, your name may have come from an ancestor who took the name from a sign in front of an inn. Or, it may have been a nickname. Or, it may have been the name given to a man because he hunted a certain kind of animal.

The names Wolf, Wolfe, Wolff, Volkov, Lowell, and Lupino all mean "wolf." Colfax, Fox, Todd, Volpe, and Voss are all names that mean "fox." Names such as Lyon, Lyons, Loewe, Leon, Singh, and Sinha mean "lion." And the names Buck, Cerf, Hart, Hirsch, Reno, Roe, and Roebuck mean "deer."

Last names such as Aguilar, Adler, Bird, Byrd, Coe, Cox, Crane, Crow, Crowe, Fasano, Garza, Gallo, Hahn, Kafka, Ortega, Poe, Velez, Vogel, and Wren come from the word *bird* or the names of different kinds of birds.

The names Haas and Hare both mean "rabbit." As you might guess, the name Baer means "bear," but so do Hong, Hung, and Xiong. Marinello means "lady bug," and Kidd means "goat." And it might surprise you to learn that the name Drake is from the word *draca*, which means "dragon"! Long and Lung mean dragon, too.

What's in a Name?   **123**

How English Came to Be

Whether you live in Australia, Canada, New Zealand, South Africa, the United Kingdom, or the United States, you most probably speak English. It's a language with an exciting history! The story of how it came to be is a story of adventure, great conquests, and terrible battles. It's a tale of people traveling to new lands in search of homes. It's a story of many different languages and how they were mixed together to make the language we call English.

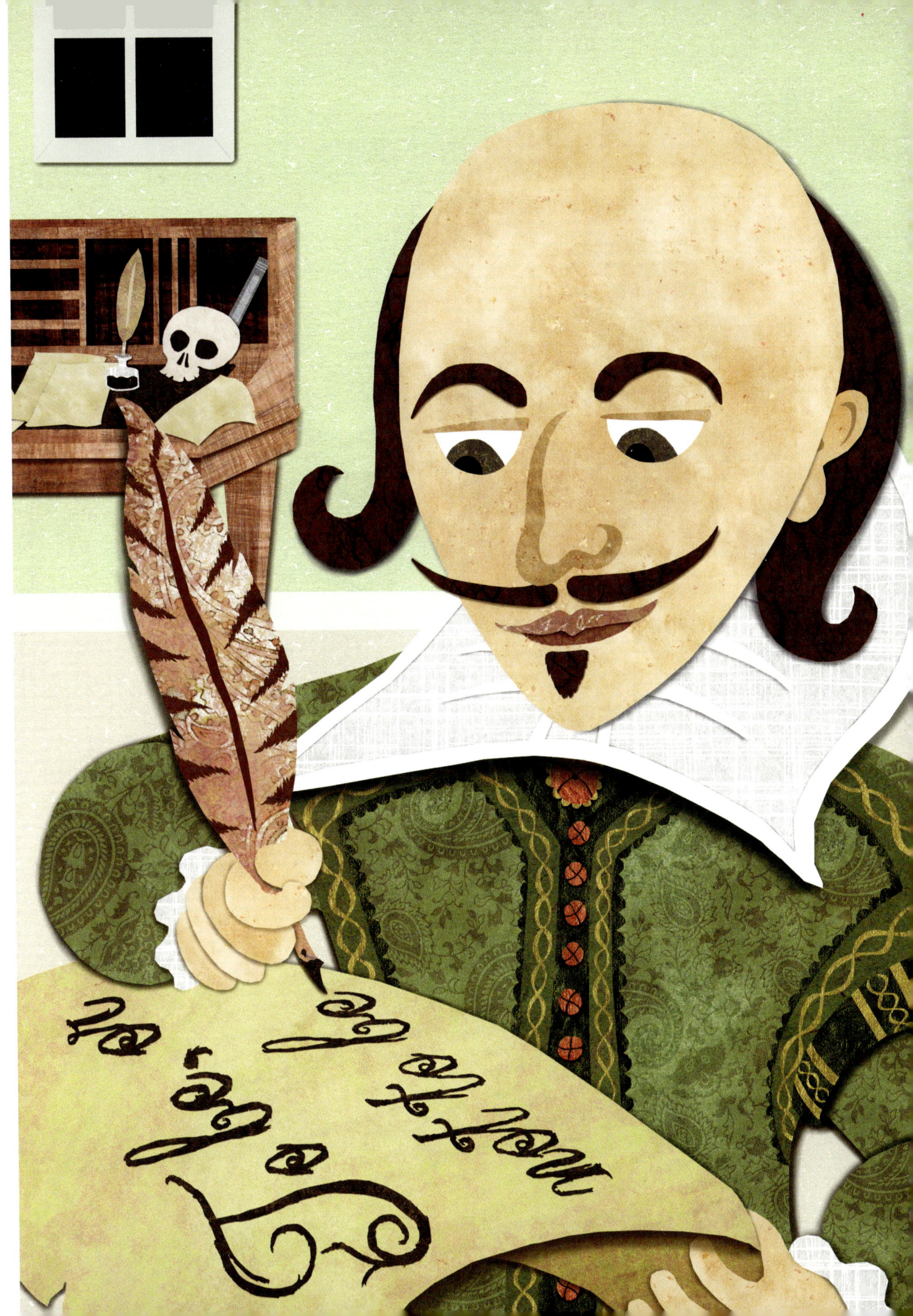
To be or not to be

From grunts to grammar

How did language begin? What were the first words? And how did we end up with so many languages?

At first, scientists believe, there were no words. Our earliest ancestors most likely made noises that meant something. A growl might have meant anger. A screech might have meant danger. A grunt might have meant food. They probably used gestures and made faces that meant things, too.

Letters to Words

As several million years passed, our ancestors began to look and act somewhat like people do today. Slowly, the first human beings began to use more and more sounds to mean things. But these sounds weren't just noises any more—they were words.

There is no way of telling what the first real words were. But scientists think they may have sounded much like the noises a baby makes before it begins to talk—sounds such as *da*, *bo*, and *muh*.

As thousands of years passed, language grew. More and more words were added. But there wasn't just one language. There were many different languages. Prehistoric people lived in little groups, often hundreds of miles apart. So language grew up in many different places—and it was different in each place.

Romans and Celts

Two thousand years ago, there was no such language as English. There wasn't even a place called England. The city of Rome, in what is now Italy, ruled much of the world. Roman armies had conquered most of Europe and large parts of Africa and the Middle East. Finally, in the year 43, a Roman army invaded a large island in the North Sea off the coast of Europe—the island that now contains England, one of the countries that make up the United Kingdom.

The land that is now England was then the home of tribes of people called Celts *(kehlts)*. The island was called Britannia, after the name of one of the tribes. It is now known as Great Britain and is part of the United Kingdom.

The Romans took over most of Britannia and ruled it for 400 years. They built military camps, forts, and roads, and they brought civilization to the Celts. Roman soldiers defended Britannia against the attacks of savage warriors called Picts, who lived in the northern part of the island.

Many Roman camps grew into towns and cities. In Latin, the Romans' language, the word for camp is *castra,* so many of the town names ended with that word. Later, *castra* became *caster, cester,* or *chester.* That's why there are many places in England with names such as Lancaster, Worcester, and Manchester. Much later, the English brought some of these names to other parts of the world.

About the year 400, Rome called all the Romans in Britannia back home to Italy, to defend their own country from invaders. When the Romans left, the story of the English language was about to begin.

The fierce warriors

The people of Britannia called themselves Britons. They spoke the Celtic and Latin languages and lived according to Roman customs. But almost as soon as the Romans were gone from Britannia, the savage Picts from the north, as well as people from Ireland called Scots, attacked!

According to tradition, Vortigern, a king of the Britons, called on warriors as fierce and savage as the Picts and Scots to help him push back the invaders. He sent word to the Angles, Saxons, and Jutes—tribes of mighty warriors who lived about where Germany is today. Soon, ships full of these hardy fighters sailed for Britannia.

For a time, the Angles, Saxons, and Jutes joined forces with the Britons. The Picts and Scots were defeated. But Britannia's troubles weren't over. The Angles and Saxons had decided to stay in Britannia and take it for themselves! More and more of these fierce warriors came to Britannia and banded together into a great army. After many years of bloody warfare, they conquered southern and eastern Britannia. They pushed the Britons into the mountains at the farthest edges of northern and western England.

After a while, Britannia became known as Angle-land. Slowly, that name was changed into England. The Angles and Saxons spoke the same language, which they called *Englisc*. We call that language Old English, or Anglo-Saxon. It was the beginning of the English language.

A cu, a docga, and a hus

What did the Old English language sound like 1,500 years ago? If you heard someone speaking it, you wouldn't understand what was being said. Old English sounds somewhat like German. A few words might sound familiar, but most would be strange.

Yet, a great many of the most common words we use every day come from the Old English language. The Anglo-Saxons used the words *and, for, in, on, to,* and *us,* just as we do. And many of the other words they used were words we now use, but they were pronounced differently.

Here are some Anglo-Saxon words that are much like the words we use:
Anglo-Saxon   cu   docga   hus   fisc   daeg
Modern English   cow   dog   house   fish   day

The way that the Anglo-Saxons put words together was a little different from the way we do, too. Here is what the first line of the Christian prayer called The Lord's Prayer looks like in Old English:

Faeder ure bu be eart on heofonum, si bin nama gehalgod.

Translated word for word, that means, "Father our, thou that art on heavens, be thy name hallowed." The Old English word *Faeder* is like our word *father; ure* is like *our;* and *nama* is like *name.* But the other words are very different from words we use today.

Letters to Words

Beowulf

One of the greatest Anglo-Saxon stories is *Beowulf*. Written in Old English, it is what is called an epic poem—a story of great adventures told in verse. *Beowulf* is considered the first great work of English literature.

The beginning of the poem looks like this in Old English:

> **Hwæt! we Gar-Dena in geardagum,**
> **þeodcyninga þrym gefrunon,**
> **hu ða æþelingas ellen fremedon!**

These words mean, "Behold! we have heard of the glory in former years of the Spear-Danes, of the kings of the people, how the heroes did brave deeds!"

The part of *Beowulf* told here has been put into Modern English. But the words, and the ways of saying things, are very much like the way the story was first written, about 1,300 years ago.

The poem tells how Hrothgar, king of the Spear-Danes, builds a splendid mead-hall, a building where his warriors eat and sleep. But the hall is haunted by Grendel, a hideous monster, half man and half beast, who lives in a nearby swamp. Whenever men sleep in the hall, Grendel breaks in to kill and eat some of them. The Danes are helpless against the terrible creature.

Then, from Sweden, comes a mighty warrior named Beowulf. He tells Hrothgar that he and his men will spend the night in the hall. He will fight Grendel and either kill the monster or die himself. This is where we begin the story.

Beowulf and Grendel

Then from his head Beowulf removed the great war helmet, and from his body the coat of armor. To a follower, he gave his brave battle sword. In pride he said, "No feebler in strength am I than Grendel. I shall not destroy him with a sword. Tonight, we shall do without weapons." Then he lay down. All slept, save he. He waited for the battle-meeting.

Then, out of the misty hills, across the moor, came Grendel stalking; he that was cursed by God. 'Neath the clouds he crept till Hrothgar's hall he saw; the gaily adorned place of feasting. Though iron bars held fast the door, the monster burst them through!

The fearsome fiend entered, eager to slay; his eyes were aglow with horrid light, like fiery coals. He saw the warriors huddled there, asleep. Filled with frightful joy was he, that now he might tear the life from every man there, feasting on their blood and bones! Yet, this was not to be. Never again would he make a man victim after this night. For a mighty warrior watched to see how the man-eater made his attack.

With a sudden spring, the monster seized a sleeper and devoured him with great, greedy bites. Then, quickly, he reached for another. But Beowulf seized his arm.

At once, the evil destroyer realized that never in all the world had he met a man of such mighty strength. Gone was his courage, and fear sat upon his heart. He wished to flee, to hide in his hole in the swamp. But Beowulf clung to him with an iron grip, clutching Grendel till his fingers cracked.

As the two foes fought, dreadful was the din. The warriors awakened and watched in fright the wild battle that shook the hall. A wonder it was that the building did not fall, so fierce was the fray as man and monster battled. The comrades of Beowulf drew their swords, eager to aid their chieftain. But the sharpest sword could not wound the creature.

Yet Grendel, who in other times had slain many men, felt now that his own body was breaking. Beowulf's grim grip was fierce upon him. The fearsome monster felt terrible pain as Beowulf tore his arm from his body. With his gaping wound, Grendel escaped. He fled across the misted moor to his dark den. Well he knew that the hours of his life had come to an end. Done were his days. From the terror of the murdering monster the Danes were saved.

How English Came to Be

The missionaries from Rome

A little more than 100 years had passed since the Angles and Saxons had conquered England. Everyone spoke the same language, but the country was divided into several small kingdoms, and the language was slightly different in each kingdom.

Ethelbert, king of one of the small kingdoms, was worried. His wife, Queen Bertha, was a Christian, but he was not. To please his wife, he had agreed to meet with a small band of Christian monks who had come from far-off Rome. But he was afraid of them. He had heard they were powerful magicians, and he feared they might enchant him.

Letters to Words

The monks approached the king, carrying a large silver cross as if it were a flag. Their leader talked to Ethelbert and explained the meaning of the Christian religion. As the king listened, his fear went away. He agreed to let the monks stay in his kingdom and preach their religion.

Soon, more and more monks came from Rome. They spoke the Latin language, which was the language of Rome and the language they used in their prayers and services. In time, the people of England began to use some Latin words. Most of the words they used had to do with religion. And that is how such words as altar, candle, cross, hymn, Mass, minister, monk, and priest came into the English language.

How English Came to Be

The coming of the Vikings

Thick, white fog drifted over the North Sea and the coast of England. There were no sounds except the screeches of gulls wheeling overhead and the hiss of waves rolling up on the shore.

Then, the silence was broken by the swish-swish-swish of oars. A fleet of long ships came sliding through the fog like lean, gray ghosts. The ships were carved and painted to look like dragons. On the ships were big, fierce warriors from the Northland. The year was 835, and the Vikings were attacking England!

For many years, England suffered terribly from the raids of the Norsemen. The Vikings sailed their ships silently along the coast, or up a river, to some unsuspecting town. Then the warriors swarmed ashore

Letters to Words

to burn the town and carry off all the treasure they could find. They also carried off people as slaves.

Many of the Vikings formed together into big armies. They conquered large parts of England and settled on the land. There was war and bloodshed for a long time, but the Vikings were much like the English people in both language and custom. Soon, the Norse and the English were living and working together, and Norsemen were marrying English women.

The Norse and English languages mixed together after a while as well. Many English words come from the language that the Vikings brought to England. Some of these words are: bank, cake, egg, give, get, husband, loan, reindeer, skin, skirt, sky, smile, and window.

The last conquest

A pale, early morning sun hung low in a gray October sky. With a clanking of armor and a clopping of horses' hoofs, the Norman army moved out to do battle against the Saxons of England.

The Normans came from Normandy, in France. Their leader was Duke William. The English king had died, and William claimed that he was supposed to be the new king. But the Saxons had made one of their leaders, Harold Godwineson, king. So William had brought his army to England to fight for the crown.

Everything depended on the battle about to be fought. If the Normans won, they would rule England. If they lost, the Saxons would show them no mercy.

On a hill near the town of Hastings, the Saxons waited. For them, too, this was an all-important battle. They were fighting for their land.

The battle raged all day. But by late afternoon it was over. Harold, the Saxon king, lay dead. The Saxons were beaten and scattered. The Normans were masters of England.

These events took place in the year 1066. Duke William, now known as William the Conqueror, became England's king. His men became barons and lords who ruled England under him. So, for about 200 years, all the kings and nobles of England spoke French. And, during this time, many French words became part of the English language.

How English Came to Be 143

New words

When you say *cow,* you're using a word from Old English. Saxon farmers who took care of the animal called it a *cu.* But when you say *beef,* you're using a word from Old French. The Norman lord who ate the *cu* for dinner called the meat *boef.*

For a long time after the Norman victory, two languages were spoken in England. The conquered Saxons spoke Old English (Anglo-Saxon). The Normans spoke Norman-French.

The Saxons were the servants and workers. This is why many of our words for everyday things come from Old English. The Normans were the lords and masters.

144   Letters to Words

This is why many of our words for fine food and clothing, and for law and government, come from Old French.

The lordly Normans ate well and in style. Some of the dining words they gave us are biscuit, cream, fruit, gravy, pork, salad, toast, veal, chair, dinner, plate, and supper. And the finely dressed Normans also gave us the words coat, dress, and fashion.

The Normans, of course, ran the government and the law courts. So such words as evidence, judge, jury, justice, mayor, parliament, and prison came from the Normans.

The language of knights and ladies

About 300 years after the Normans invaded England, people no longer called themselves Normans or Saxons—now they were all English. There were castles and tournaments, knights in shining armor, and ladies in fancy gowns. And the people spoke a language that had slowly grown out of Old English and Norman-French. We call this language Middle English.

Middle English was much more like the kind of English we speak than was Old English. But even so, you wouldn't be able to understand much of it if you saw it written or heard it spoken. Many Middle English words are no longer used. Even those that are still used are now spelled and pronounced differently.

When we use the word *bite*, we say *byt*. But people who spoke Middle English would have said *beet* or *beet uh*. For *about*, we say *uh bowt*. In Middle English, it was *uh boot*. For *done*, we say *duhn*. In Middle English, it was *duhn uh*.

Middle English was spoken from about 1100 to 1500. That was a time of romance and adventure. Many wonderful poems and stories, such as those about Robin Hood and King Arthur, were first written down then.

The Canterbury Tales

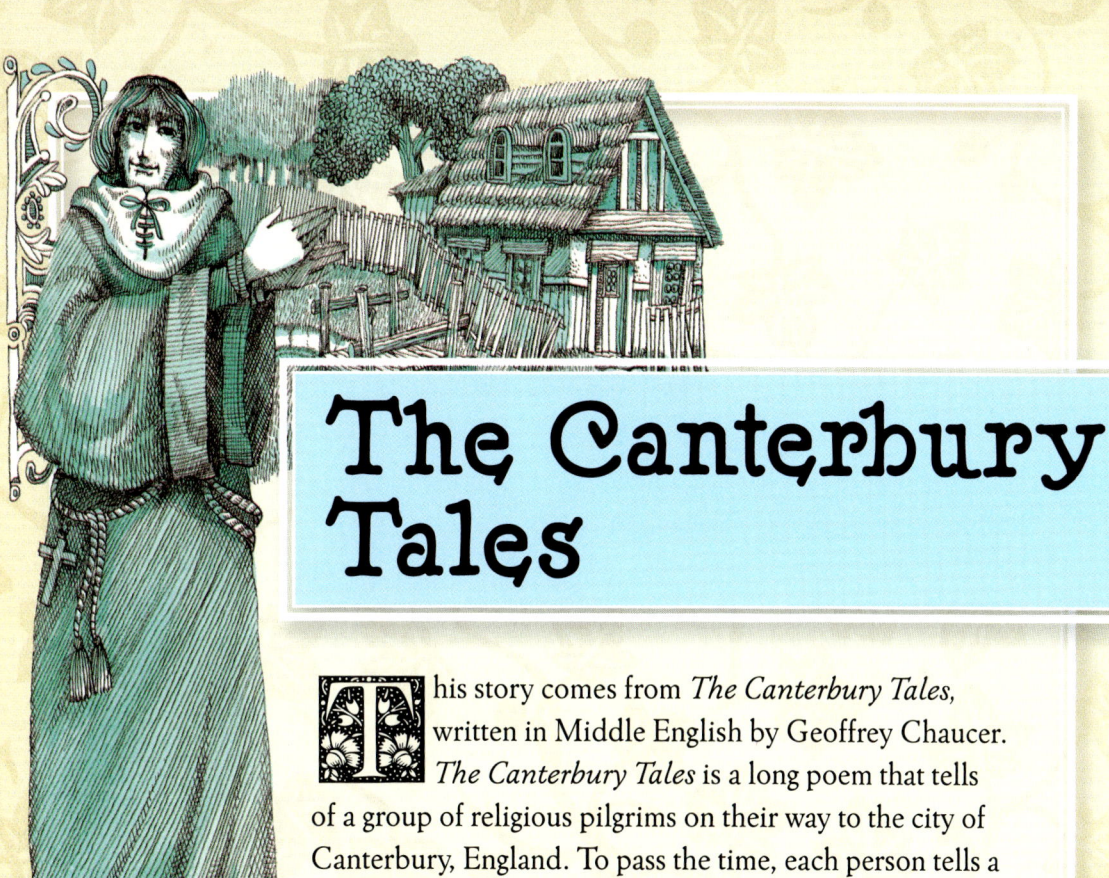

This story comes from *The Canterbury Tales*, written in Middle English by Geoffrey Chaucer. *The Canterbury Tales* is a long poem that tells of a group of religious pilgrims on their way to the city of Canterbury, England. To pass the time, each person tells a story. A priest tells the story of Chauntecleer.

You would not understand many of the words in the original. Here, for example, are the first three lines as Chaucer wrote them in Middle English, with the Modern English words underneath:

A povre wydwe, somdeel stape in age
(A poor widow, somewhat advanced in age)
Was whilom dwelling in a narwe cottage,
(Was once dwelling in a small cottage,)
Biside a grove, stondynge in a dale.
(Beside a grove, standing in a dale.)

In this retelling, modern spelling has been used. However, the sentences have been kept much the way Chaucer wrote them, and the expressions are much like the ones he used.

How English Came to Be

Chauntecleer and the Fox

A poor widow, growing rather old, once dwelt in a small cottage beside a grove standing in a valley. This widow, of whom I tell you my tale, had patiently led a very simple life since the day her husband died. By taking care of what God gave her, she made a living for herself and her two daughters. She had only three large sows, three cows, and a sheep called Moll.

Quite dingy was her bedroom, and also her dining room, in which she ate many a slim meal. Spicy sauces she never needed, for no dainty snacks passed through her throat. Her meals were as plain as her coat. No wine drank she, neither white nor red. Her table was set mostly with white and black—milk and brown bread—of which she had no lack. And sometimes there was broiled bacon and an egg or two.

She had a yard that was enclosed all about with a fence of sticks and a ditch. There she kept a rooster called Chauntecleer. In all the land, for crowing none was his equal. His voice was merrier than the merry organ that plays on Mass days in the church. More dependable than a clock was his crowing. The comb on his head was redder than fine coral. His bill was black, and like jet it shone. Like azure were his legs and toes, with nails whiter than the lily flowers. And like polished gold was the color of his body.

This noble rooster had in his care seven hens that were wondrously like him in color. The prettiest of these was called the fair lady Pertelote. Polite she was, careful and charming and good-natured. And truly, she had hold of the heart of Chauntecleer. He loved her well and was most happy. It was a joy to hear them sing together when the bright sun shone in spring. For in those days, so I understand, beasts and birds could speak and sing.

It happened that early one morning as Chauntecleer slept on his perch among the hens, he gave a groan deep in his throat. When Pertelote heard him she was startled and said, "Sweetheart, what ails you, that you groan so?"

And he answered, saying, "My Lady, I dreamed that I was in such trouble that

How English Came to Be

my heart is filled with fear! It seemed that while I roamed up and down within our yard I saw a strange beast that was like a dog, and that tried to capture me and would have killed me. His color was a cross between red and yellow, and his tail and ears with black were tipped. He had a small snout and two gleaming eyes that looked at me so fearsomely I nearly died of fright. No doubt this frightful dream caused my groaning."

"Shame!" cried she. "I cannot love a coward, by my faith! How dare you say that anything has made you afraid? How can you have been afraid of a dream?"

"I tell you, pretty Pertelote," said Chauntecleer, "that some dreams are to be feared. They are warnings of things that may happen. But let us speak of happy things, and forget all this. For when I see the beauty of your face, so rosy-red around the eyes, it makes my fear die."

With those words he flew down from his perch, for it was now daytime. He clucked whenever he found some corn, and then the hens came running to his call. Then, as he walked, he cast up his eyes at the sun and knew that it was spring. Joyfully he crowed, "My Lady Pertelote, hear how the happy birds sing, and see how the flowers spring up. Full is my heart of joy!"

But soon he was in great trouble, for all joy ends in sorrow.

A sly and wicked fox, with black-tipped ears and tail, had broken through the fence in the night. And in a flower bed he lay, waiting his chance to seize Chauntecleer. Oh, poor Chauntecleer, this is what you were warned of in your dream!

As Chauntecleer walked, singing, he cast his eye on a butterfly among the flowers and saw the fox, crouching there.

He would have fled, but the fox quickly said, "Noble sir, where are you going? Be you afraid of me, that am your friend? I am only here to listen to you sing, for truly, you have as fine a voice as any angel.

"Your father, God bless his soul, and your gentle mother have been in my house, to my delight. And I will say that, save for you, I never heard a man sing as did your father in the morning. Truly, his every song 'twas from the heart. So that his voice might be stronger, he would close both eyes and, standing on tiptoe, he would stretch his neck until it was long and thin. Now sing, Sir, and let us see if you can match your father."

Then Chauntecleer began to flap his wings, so pleased was he by all this flattery.

Ah! Take care all you great people! There is many a flatterer in your palaces, and many a trickster who cares more to fool you than he does for truth and rightness. Beware, my lords, of all their treachery!

Then Chauntecleer stood high upon his toes, stretched out his neck, closed his eyes, and began to crow with all his might.

How English Came to Be

At once the fox grabbed Chauntecleer by the throat! Flinging Chauntecleer over his shoulder, he rushed back toward the woods.

Alas that Chauntecleer flew down from his perch this day! Alas that his wife paid no attention to his dream!

Great was the cry of the hens when they saw Chauntecleer carried off. And Pertelote cried loudest.

The widow and her daughters heard the noise and ran from the house. Seeing the fox heading into the woods, they ran after him crying, "Help! Help! The fox!" And after them came men with sticks, and dogs, and other women. The cows and the sows and the sheep, frightened by the barking of the dogs, ran after the men and women. Frightened geese flew up into the air and a swarm of bees came out of their hive. Such was the noise they all made, it seemed that heaven would fall down.

Now, good people, I pray you to listen. See how luck can change. For, in spite of his fear, Chauntecleer, who lay across the fox's back, did say, "Sir, if I were you I would say, 'Turn back, you interfering, ignorant clods! May a sickness fall upon you all! This rooster shall be mine in spite of you. I'll eat him, by my faith, and at once!'"

The fox answered, "By my faith, it shall be done." And the instant he opened his mouth to say this, Chauntecleer pulled his neck from the fox's teeth and broke free. Up into a tree he flew.

When the fox realized Chauntecleer was gone he said, "Oh, Chauntecleer, alas! I have done you a great wrong by frightening you when I took you out of the yard. But sir, I did not intend any wickedness. Come down, and I shall tell you what I meant."

"Nay, then," said Chauntecleer. "May I curse myself if I let you trick me more than once. Never again will flattery get me to sing and close my eyes. For he who shuts his eyes when he ought to look, may God let him never be free."

"Nay," said the fox, "but may God give bad luck to him who is so careless that he chatters when he should keep closed his mouth."

Now you who think this is just a foolish story of rooster, hen, and fox, do not overlook the wisdom that is in it. For all that is written is written to tell some useful truth. Take the truth and leave the rest.

The age of Elizabeth

*Spring, the sweet spring, is the year's pleasant king;
Then blooms each thing, then maids dance in a ring,
Cold doth not sting, the pretty birds do sing....*

You can easily understand that poem. Every word in it but one—doth—is a word we use today. The poem was written in 1592, when English was not too different from the English we speak now. England was then ruled by Queen Elizabeth I. We call that time the Elizabethan Age.

English in the Elizabethan Age was not exactly like Modern English. There were still many differences. Some words were pronounced differently—a word such as *bite* was pronounced *bayt*. And words such as *does* and *has* were spoken and written as *doth* and *hath*. Instead of *you* and *your*, people said *thou* and *thy*.

The people of Elizabethan England were fond of plays, poetry, and music. Some of the greatest English poems and plays were written during that time. The greatest playwright of all time, William Shakespeare, lived during the Elizabethan Age. The many wonderful plays he wrote are still performed.

A Midsummer Night's Dream

William Shakespeare wrote the play *A Midsummer Night's Dream* about 1595. It is a fun-filled story about fairies, strange happenings, and enchantments.

Most of the play takes place in a woods where Oberon and Titania, king and queen of the fairies, are staying with all their elves, sprites, and goblins. A group of rather foolish men come to the woods at night to practice a play in secret. Shakespeare gave these men names that still make people chuckle—such names as Quince, Snug, Bottom, Flute, Snout, and Starveling.

As the men practice, a mischievous elf named Puck enchants Bottom and gives him the head of an ass, which is what a donkey was usually called in Shakespeare's time. Bottom does not know he has been enchanted. But when the other men see him they are terrified and run away.

Meanwhile, Titania, the fairy queen, has been sleeping nearby. She, too, has been enchanted so that she will fall in love with the first creature she sees when she awakens. And the first one she sees is Bottom, with his ass's head!

Here, then, is part of the play, just as Shakespeare wrote it more than 400 years ago. Some of the words and sayings will seem strange. These have been numbered. As you come to them, you'll find them explained at the *foot* (bottom) of the page.

How English Came to Be 155

Nick Bottom and the Fairies

Bottom: Why do they run away? This is a knavery[1] of them to make me afeard[2].

Re-enter Snout

Snout: O Bottom, thou art changed! What do I see on thee?

Bottom: What do you see? You see an ass-head of your own, do you? [*Exit* Snout]

Re-enter Quince

Quince: Bless thee, Bottom! Bless thee! Thou art translated[3]. *[Exit]*

Bottom: I see their knavery. This is to make an ass of me; to frighten me, if they could. But I will not stir from this place, do what they can. I will walk up and down here, and I will sing, that they shall hear I am not afraid. *[Sings]*

    The ousel cock[4] so black of hue,
    With orange-tawny bill,
    The throstle[5] with his note so true,
    The wren will little quill,—

Titania: *[Awakening]* What angel wakes me from my flowery bed?

Bottom: *[Sings]*

    The finch, the sparrow, and the lark,
    The plain-song cuckoo gray,
    Whose note full many a man doth mark,[6]
    And dares not answer nay;—

For, indeed, who would set his wit to so foolish a bird?[7] Who would give a bird the lie, though he cry 'cuckoo' never so?[8]

---

1. trick
2. afraid
3. changed
4. male blackbird
5. thrush
6. whose singing many men notice
7. Who would bother with such a foolish bird?
8. Who would call a bird a liar just because it called "cuckoo" over and over?

How English Came to Be   157

Titania: I pray thee, gentle mortal, sing again.
Mine ear is much enamour'd of thy note;[9]
So is mine eye enthralled to thy shape;[10]
And they fair virtue's force perforce doth move me[11]
On the first view to say, to swear, I love thee.

Bottom: Methinks, mistress, you should have little reason for that. And yet, to say the truth, reason and love keep little company together now-a-days. The more the pity that some honest neighbors will not make them friends. Nay, I can gleek upon occasion.[12]

Titania: Thou art as wise as thou art beautiful.

Bottom: Not so, neither; but if I had wit enough to get out of this wood, I have enough to serve mine own turn.

---

9. I'm in love with your singing.
10. My eyes are pleased with your looks.
11. The power of your beauty moves me.
12. I can joke at times.

Titania: Out of this wood do not desire to go.
    Thou shalt remain here, whether thou wilt or no.
    I am a spirit of no common rate,
    The summer still doth tend upon my state;[13]
    And I do love thee. Therefore, go with me.
    I'll give thee fairies to attend on thee,
    And they shall fetch thee jewels from the deep,
    And sing while thou on pressed flowers dost sleep:
    And I will purge thy mortal grossness so
    That thou shalt like an airy spirit go.[14]
    Peaseblossom! Cobweb! Moth! And Mustardseed!

Enter Peaseblossom, Cobweb, Moth, *and* Mustardseed

Peaseblossom: Ready.

---

13. It is always summer in my Kingdom.
14. I will change your heavy, human body so that you will be like an invisible spirit.

How English Came to Be

Cobweb: And I.

Moth: And I.

Mustardseed: And I.

All: Where shall we go?

Titania: Be kind and courteous to this gentleman.
      Hop in his walks and gambol in his eyes;
      Feed him with apricocks and dewberries,
      With purple grapes, green figs, and mulberries;
      The honey-bags steal from the humble-bees,
      And for night-tapers crop their waxen thighs,[15]
      And light them at the fiery glow-worm's eyes,
      To have my love to bed and to arise;
      And pluck the wings from painted butterflies
      To fan the moonbeams from his sleeping eyes.
      Nod to him, elves, and do him courtesies.

Peaseblossom: Hail, mortal!

Cobweb: Hail!

Moth: Hail!

Mustardseed: Hail!

15. for candles, cut off their waxy legs.

How English Came to Be

Words from everywhere

During the Elizabethan Age, the English explored the Caribbean Islands and parts of North and South America. And English merchants carried on more and more trade with the Far East. By the 1700's, English ports were crowded with ships bringing back goods, treasures—and new words—from many parts of the world.

For hundreds of years, the English language had borrowed words from other languages. Now, many more new words—for new foods, new kinds of clothing, and new animals—were brought back to England.

Sometimes these new words came straight into English from the foreign language. The word *volcano,* for example, came directly into English from Italian. At other times the English word was picked up from the French or Spanish version of a foreign word. On the next two pages are some of the many English words borrowed from other languages.

Letters to Words

Italy
balcony
bandit
carnival
influenza
macaroni
piano
rocket
studio
violin
zucchini

The Netherlands
easel
landscape
skate
sleigh

Portugal
marmalade
molasses

Spain
banana
canyon
guitar
mosquito
patio
tornado
vanilla

Russia
czar
mammoth

India
bandanna
bungalow
guru
jungle
madras
pajamas
polo
shampoo

China
tea
tycoon

Japan
haiku
karate
kimono
samurai

Malaya (an area in what is now Malaysia)
bamboo
caddy
gingham
orangutan

Arabia (an area in what is now Saudi Arabia)
admiral
assassin
coffee
magazine
syrup
zero

Iran (formerly known as Persia)
bazaar
magic
paradise
shawl
tiger

macaroni

guitar

karate

bamboo

tiger

How English Came to Be 163

igloo

canoe

Africa
gorilla
jazz
safari
voodoo
zebra

Australian Aborigines
boomerang
kangaroo
koala

Inuit *(a people once called Eskimos)*
igloo
kayak

Aztec Indians
chocolate

American Indians
bullfrog
chipmunk
moccasin
moose
raccoon
toboggan

Caribbean Islands
barbecue
canoe
hammock
hurricane
potato
tobacco

By the middle of the 1800's, all these words were part of the English language. People were now saying *you, your,* and *yours* instead of *thee, thy,* and *thine.* And they no longer said *doth* and *hath* for *does* and *has.* English was very much like it is today.

boomerang

Letters to Words

A Christmas Carol

The story below is part of a wonderful book called *A Christmas Carol* by the English author Charles Dickens. It was written in 1843. Most of the words that people used then are still used. But some of them may be new to you. When you come to a word you don't understand, look it up in the dictionary. Then you'll know a new word.

Some of the expressions that people used then are no longer used. These have been numbered. As you come to them, you'll find them explained at the bottom of the page.

In this part of the story, the family of Bob Cratchit, a poor clerk, is getting ready to have Christmas dinner.

How English Came to Be

Christmas at the Cratchits'

Then up rose Mrs. Cratchit, Cratchit's wife, dressed out but poorly in a twice-turned gown[1], but brave in ribbons[2], which are cheap and make a goodly show for sixpence[3]; and she laid the cloth[4], assisted by Belinda Cratchit, second of her daughters, also brave in ribbons; while Master Peter Cratchit plunged a fork into the saucepan of potatoes, and getting the corners of his monstrous shirt collar (Bob's private property, conferred upon his son and heir in honour of the day) into his mouth, rejoiced to find himself so gallantly attired, and yearned to show his linen in the fashionable Parks[5]. And now two smaller Cratchits, boy and girl, came tearing in, screaming that outside the baker's they had smelt the goose, and known it for their own[6]; and basking in luxurious thoughts of sage and onion, these young Cratchits danced about the table, and exalted Master Peter Cratchit to the skies, while he (not proud, although his collars nearly choked him) blew the fire until the slow potatoes bubbling up, knocked loudly at the saucepan-lid to be let out and peeled.

"What has ever got your precious father, then?[7]" said Mrs. Cratchit. "And your brother, Tiny Tim! And Martha warn't as late last Christmas Day by half-an-hour![8]"

---

1. a dress that had been remade twice.
2. decorated with many ribbons.
3. a fine appearance, costing very little.
4. set the table.
5. He wished to show off his clothes among the wealthy people in the parks.
6. The Cratchits, like other poor families, had no oven; the neighborhood baker was roasting their goose in his big oven.
7. "What has delayed your father?"
8. Martha arrived half an hour earlier last Christmas.

"Here's Martha, mother!" said a girl, appearing as she spoke.

"Here's Martha, mother!" cried the two young Cratchits. "Hurrah! There's *such* a goose, Martha!"

"Why, bless your heart alive, my dear, how late you are!" said Mrs. Cratchit, kissing her a dozen times, and taking off her shawl and bonnet for her with officious zeal.

"We'd a deal of work to finish up last night," replied the girl, "and had to clear away this morning, mother!"

"Well! Never mind so long as you are come," said Mrs. Cratchit. "Sit ye down before the fire, my dear, and have a warm, Lord bless ye!"

"No, no! There's father coming," cried the two young Cratchits, who were everywhere at once. "Hide, Martha, hide!"

So Martha hid herself, and in came little Bob, the father, with at least three feet of comforter exclusive of the fringe[9] hanging down before him; and his threadbare clothes darned up and brushed, to look seasonable; and Tiny Tim upon his shoulder. Alas for Tiny Tim, he bore a little crutch and had his limbs supported by an iron frame![10]

"Why, where's our Martha?" cried Bob Cratchit, looking round.

"Not coming," said Mrs. Cratchit.

"Not coming!" said Bob, with a sudden declension in his high spirits; for he had been Tim's blood horse all the way from church and had come home rampant[11]. "Not coming upon Christmas Day!"

---

9. three feet of woolen scarf, not counting the fringe.
10. He had metal braces on his legs.
11. He had carried Tiny Tim on his shoulders, pretending to be a very fine horse, and had come home quite excited.

Martha didn't like to see him disappointed, if it were only in joke; so she came out prematurely from behind the closed door, and ran into his arms, while the two young Cratchits hustled Tiny Tim, and bore him off into the wash-house, that he might hear the pudding singing in the copper[12].

"And how did little Tim behave?" asked Mrs. Cratchit, when she had rallied Bob on his credulity[13] and Bob had hugged his daughter to his heart's content.

"As good as gold," said Bob, "and better. Somehow he gets thoughtful sitting by himself so much, and thinks the strangest things you ever heard. He told me coming home, that he hoped

---

12. the sound of the plum pudding steaming in a large copper pot.
13. She teased Bob for believing Martha wasn't there.

the people saw him in the church, because he was a cripple, and it might be pleasant to them to remember upon Christmas Day, who made lame beggars walk and blind men see."

Bob's voice was tremulous when he told them this, and trembled more when he said that Tiny Tim was growing strong and hearty.

His active little crutch was heard upon the floor, and back came Tiny Tim before another word was spoken, escorted by his brother and sister to his stool before the fire; and while Bob, turning up his cuffs—as if, poor fellow, they were capable of being made more shabby—compounded some hot mixture in a jug with gin and lemons, and stirred it round and round and put it on the hob to simmer; Master Peter and the two ubiquitous young Cratchits went to fetch the goose, with which they soon returned in high procession[14].

---

14. like a parade.

Such a bustle ensued that you might have thought a goose the rarest of all birds; a feathered phenomenon, to which a black swan was a matter of course—and in truth it was something very like it in that house[15]. Mrs. Cratchit made the gravy (ready beforehand in a little saucepan) hissing hot; Master Peter mashed the potatoes with incredible vigour; Miss Belinda sweetened up the applesauce; Martha dusted the hot plates; Bob took Tiny Tim beside him in a tiny corner at the table; the two young Cratchits set chairs for everybody, not forgetting themselves, and mounting guard upon their posts[16] crammed spoons into their mouths lest they should shriek for goose before their turn came to be helped. At last the dishes were set on, and grace was said. It was succeeded by a breathless pause, as Mrs. Cratchit, looking slowly all along the

---

15. A goose dinner for the Cratchits was more rare than a black swan.
16. sitting at their places at the table.

carving knife, prepared to plunge it in the breast; but when she did, and when the long expected gush of stuffing issued forth, one murmur of delight arose all around the board, and even Tiny Tim, excited by the two young Cratchits, beat on the table with the handle of his knife, and feebly cried Hurrah!

There never was such a goose. Bob said he didn't believe there ever was such a goose cooked. Its tenderness and flavour, size and cheapness, were the themes of universal admiration. Eked out[17] by the applesauce and mashed potatoes, it was a sufficient dinner for the whole family; indeed, as Mrs. Cratchit said with great delight (surveying one small atom of a bone upon the dish) they hadn't ate it all at last! Yet everyone had had enough, and the youngest Cratchits in particular were steeped in sage and onion to the eyebrows! But now, the plates being changed by Miss Belinda, Mrs. Cratchit left the room alone—too nervous to bear witnesses—to take the plum pudding up and bring it in.

Suppose it should not be done enough! Suppose it should break in turning out! Suppose somebody should have got over the wall of the backyard, and stolen it, while they were merry with the goose—a supposition at which the two young Cratchits became livid! All sorts of horrors were supposed.

Hallo! A great deal of steam! The pudding was out of the copper. A smell like washing-day! That was the cloth[18]. A smell like an eating-house and pastry cook's next door to each other, with a laundress's next door to that! That was the pudding! In half a minute Mrs. Cratchit entered—flushed, but smiling proudly—with the pudding, like a speckled cannonball, so hard and firm, blazing in half of half-a-quartern[19] of ignited brandy, and bedight with Christmas holly stuck into the top.

---

17. added to.
18. The pudding was covered with a cloth to keep the warmth and steam in.
19. A quartern is equal to four ounces, so there was only one ounce of brandy on the pudding—a very small amount.

Oh, a wonderful pudding! Bob Cratchit said, and calmly too, that he regarded it as the greatest success achieved by Mrs. Cratchit since their marriage. Mrs. Cratchit said that now the weight was off her mind, she would confess she had had her doubts about the quantity of flour. Everybody had something to say about it, but nobody said or thought it was at all a small pudding for a large family. It would have been flat heresy to do so. Any Cratchit would have blushed to hint at such a thing.

At last the dinner was all done, the cloth was cleared, the hearth swept, and the fire made up. The compound in the jug being tasted, and considered perfect, apples and oranges were put upon the table, and a shovelful of chestnuts on the fire[20]. Then all the Cratchit family drew around the hearth, in what Bob Cratchit called a circle, meaning half a one; and at Bob's elbow stood the family display of glass[21]. Two tumblers and a custard-cup without a handle.

These held the hot stuff from the jug, however, as well as golden goblets would have done; and Bob served it out with beaming looks, while the chestnuts on the fire sputtered and cracked noisily. Then Bob proposed:—

"A Merry Christmas to us all, my dears. God bless us!"

Which all the family re-echoed.

"God bless us every one!" said Tiny Tim, the last of all.

---

20. Roast chestnuts were a favorite snack.
21. the family's drinking glasses.

English

Explorers and Traders

Vikings

Angles, Saxons, and Jutes

Still going—

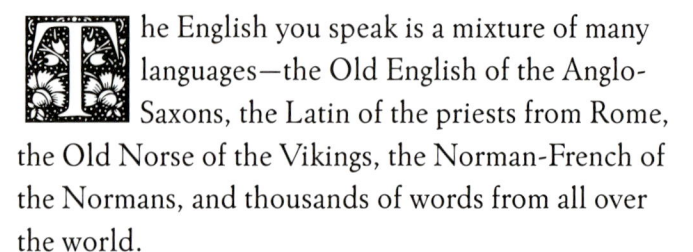

The English you speak is a mixture of many languages—the Old English of the Anglo-Saxons, the Latin of the priests from Rome, the Old Norse of the Vikings, the Norman-French of the Normans, and thousands of words from all over the world.

Two thousand years ago, there was no such thing as the English language. But today, English is spoken by more people than any other language, either as a

still growing

primary (first or main) language or as a secondary language. About 400 million people speak English as their native language. English is the primary language of the people of Australia, most of Canada, Ireland, New Zealand, South Africa, the United Kingdom, the United States, and about 30 small island nations. It is used as an official language by more than 50 other nations. Altogether, nearly 2 billion people speak at least a little English.

All Kinds of English

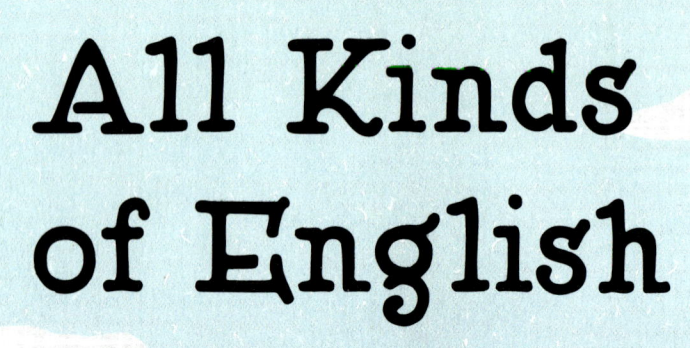

Millions of people in many parts of the world speak English as their everyday language. But they don't all speak it the same way. People in different places use some different words and often pronounce and spell words in different ways. What kind of English do you speak? You may be surprised to find how different your English is from the English spoken somewhere else.

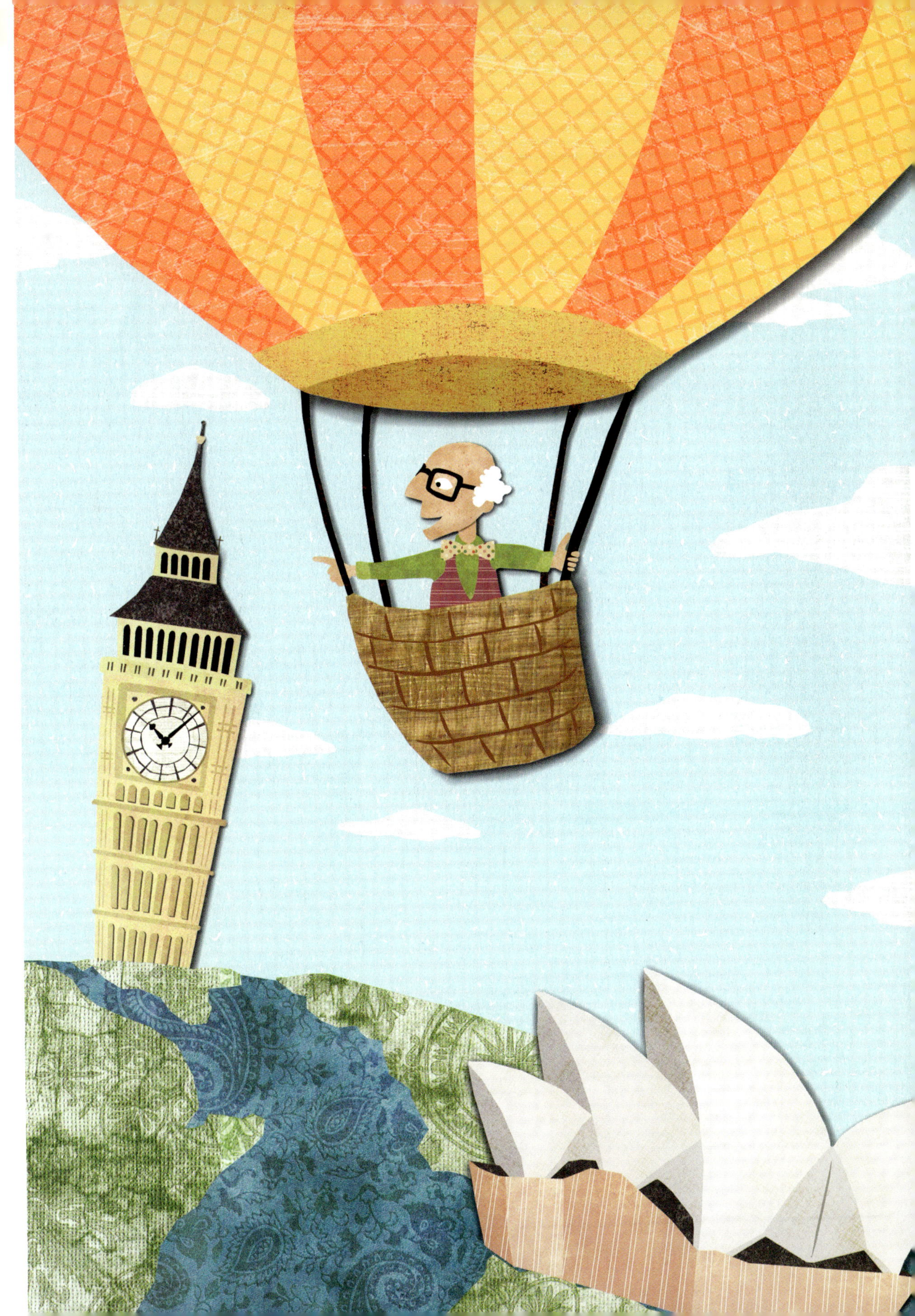

Other places, other

The English girl said, "I'm mad about my flat!" Her American friend nodded. "I'd be angry, too, if I'd had a flat tire." But what the English girl meant was that she really liked her apartment.

For a long time after British colonists began settling in North America in the 1600's, they spoke the same kind of English that people "back home" in England did. But over time, the kind of English spoken in the United States changed, as Americans adapted to their new country and to colonists from other lands. Today, there are times when the British and Americans are confused by one another's words. Sometimes, the same word means quite different things. To the British, football means a game Americans call soccer— a game quite different from American football. And sometimes the same things have different names:

football / soccer

trolley / shopping cart

British	American
chips	French fries
crisps	potato chips
biscuits	cookies
lift	elevator
bonnet (of a car)	hood
boot (of a car)	trunk
trolley (in a supermarket)	shopping cart
draughts	checkers
mobile	cell phone

Letters to Words

words

English words may mean something different in Australia, as well. An Australian boy said, "My father runs a station." His American friend thought the father ran a gas station. But the Australian meant a sheep ranch. So the same thing can have three different names in British, Australian, and American English!

British	Australian	American
sweets	lollies	candy
mate	cobber (cob) or mate	friend (buddy or pal)
vest	singlet	tank top
flat	unit	apartment
petrol station	servo	gas station
fizzy drink	lolly water	soda (pop)
trainers	joggers	sneakers (gym shoes)

People in different parts of the United States also have different names for some things. If you want a soft drink in the Northwest or Midwest, ask for a *pop*. In the Northeast, the Southwest, and the St. Louis, Missouri, area, you would say *soda*. But in the South, you would ask for a *Coke* even if you wanted a root beer!

All Kinds of English

Have you ever played a sidewalk game called *hopscotch?* Or do you call it *potsy* or *sky blue?* At the playground, do you ride on a seesaw or a teeter-totter? Do you fish in a creek, a brook, or a branch? And do you fry up your catch in a frying pan, a spider, or a skillet?

No matter where you live, you almost certainly use some slang words. Slang is the name we give to informal words that may be made up or just used in a special way for a time. There are slang words in every language and every country. If you say that someone is chicken—meaning afraid—you're using American slang. If you say that someone is bonkers—meaning nutty or goofy—you're using British slang. And if you call someone fair dinkum—meaning honest or true—you're using Australian slang.

Australian English contains many slang words, as well as words from the language of the Aborigines, the native people of Australia. Here is a verse from the famous Australian song "Waltzing Matilda."

> Once a jolly swagman camped by a billabong,
> Under the shade of a coolabah tree;
> And he sang as he watched and waited 'till his billy boiled,
> "You'll come a-waltzing Matilda with me!"

If you're not an Australian, you may not understand all the words. What's a *swagman?* What's a *billabong?*

A swagman carries his billy and Matilda as he goes a-waltzing.

Letters to Words

A swagman is a wanderer—a tramp or a hobo. Billabong is from an Aboriginal word meaning "branch of a river." A billy is a tin can in which the swagman boils his tea over a campfire. Matilda is not a girl, but a rolled-up blanket in which the swagman keeps his swag, or belongings. And to go waltzing means "to go for a walk or a tramp."

The people who live in one part of the city of London, England, are called cockneys. Cockneys have a special kind of rhyming slang. They may say "trouble and strife" instead of *wife*, "plates of meat" for *feet*, "apples and pears" for *stairs*, "loaf of bread" for *head*, or "mince pies" for *eyes*. This kind of slang is even harder to understand when it is shortened, so that *loaf* stands for *head* and *minces* for *eyes*.

What do you say when you want someone to go away? An American might say "Get lost!" But a cockney would say " 'Op it!"

Slang is always changing. In the late 1800's, if an American were asked to do something he didn't want to do, he'd probably have said, "Not on your tintype!" In the early 1900's, he might have said, "Not a chance!" Today, a common answer might be "No way!" What will it be next?

Slang makes language very colorful and interesting. But too much slang "covers up" the language and makes it hard for people to understand one another. And there is no point in telling someone to " 'Op it!" if he or she doesn't understand what " 'Op it!" means!

Not on your tintype!

Not a chance!

No way!

All Kinds of English **181**

Other places, other

How do you say the word *again?* How you say it depends on where you live or how you've learned to say it. Most people in Canada and the United States say *uh gehn*. But in the New England States, many people say *uh gan*. In the Southern States, most people usually say *uh gihn*, as do many people in Scotland and Ireland. Many people in England say *uh gayn*. But in parts of England and Australia, some people say *uh gyn*.

The way people say words is part of what is called dialect. Most people call it accent. We say that someone speaks with a Southern accent, or an English accent, or whatever kind of accent. We usually think of other people as having an accent. But everyone speaks with some kind of accent.

There are three main accents in the United States. The most common accent is called General American. This is what you hear in most of the West, the Midwest, and parts of the East. If you go to the South or Southwest, you will hear a Southern accent. And in the Northeast, you will hear a New England accent. Within these areas you will also hear other accents.

About three out of four Americans have a General American accent. In this accent, the *r* is always heard. Most Americans say *bawrd* for *board*. But many New Englanders say *bawd* and most Southerners say *bohd*.

182 Letters to Words

sounds

New Englanders often speak with a broad *a*, so that many words have an *ah* sound. They say *fahst* for *fast* and *pahth* for *path*. They also drop the *r* sound, pronouncing *farm* as *fahm* and *car* as *cah*. And if a word ends with an *ah* or *aw* sound, they often use an *r* sound, saying *sawr* for *saw*.

In the South and Southwest, most people have a Southern accent. They stretch out vowel sounds and drop their *r*'s. They say *suh* for *sir*, *Ah* for *I*, and *doah* for *door*.

In the United Kingdom, there are some two dozen dialects. Even in England alone there are many dialects. For the word *heart*, you will hear *hurt* in Lancashire, *hawrt* in Devonshire, *hairt* in Northumberland, and *ahrt* among the cockneys of London. How do you say the words *clerk, schedule, and vitamin?* Many people in the United Kingdom and Canada say *klahrk, shehd yool,* and *vih tuh mihn*. But most people in the United States say *klurk, skehj ule,* and *vy tuh mihn*.

A person who speaks with a strong Australian accent says *lydee* for *lady*, *iht* for *hit*, and *dy* for day. When you hear Australians say, " 'Owyergoin' mateorright?" they mean "How are you going (doing) mate (buddy), all right?" And in New Zealand, people seem to say *uht uhz* for *it is*. Many people in Canada speak with an accent that is much like General American. But Canadians may give an *oo* sound to words that have *ou* in them. They often say *oot* for *out* and *aboot* for *about*.

So, what kind of accent do you have? How do you say *log* and *dog*, or *cot* and *caught*, or *marry, Mary,* and *merry?* When you say the word *greasy*, do you say *greesee* or *greezee?* When you ask for a drink of water, do you ask for *wawter* or *wahter?* Try listening to yourself and others. You will soon discover many differences in the way people say words.

All Kinds of English

How to spell fish

Do you think you know how to spell *fish?* Well, think again. We usually spell a word by the sounds in the word. But English is full of different letter combinations that have the same sounds. If you listen to the sounds in *fish* and remember the wrong letter combinations, you might end up with *ghoti!*

Impossible? Not at all. Take the *f* sound of *gh* in *enough (ih nuhf)*, the *i* sound of *o* in *women (wihm uhn)* and the *sh* sound of *ti* in nation *(nay shuhn)* and you get *ghoti*, not *fish*. Can you think of strange ways to spell other words?

There was a time when people spelled words just about any way they wanted to. But it is easier if we all spell words the same way. This is one reason for dictionaries. But even with dictionaries, we still don't all use the same spelling for many words.

If you love to read, you may have found this out for yourself. The fact is, the British and Americans spell some words quite differently. And Australians and Canadians use many British spellings. On the following page are a few examples of the differences in British and American spellings you may see in books:

Letters to Words

British	American
centre	center
colour	color
tyre	tire
connexion	connection
kerb	curb
waggon	wagon
gaol	jail
defence	defense
cheque	check
plough	plow
draught	draft
aluminium	aluminum

All Kinds of English

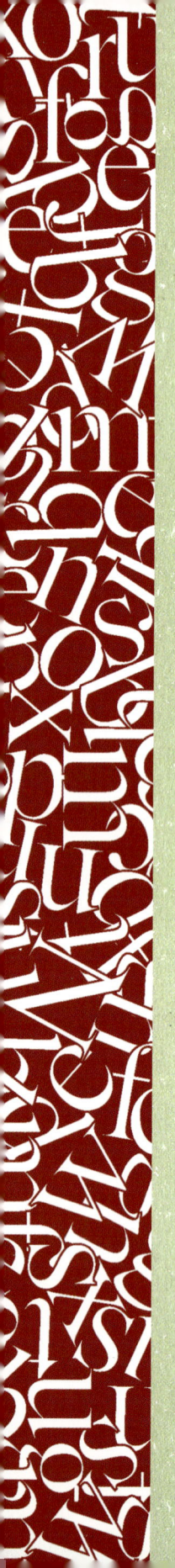

Fun with Words

Did you ever stop to think how many games, puzzles, and other ways of having fun depend on words? Here are a few word games. See for yourself how much fun you can have with words! And how much you can learn while having fun!

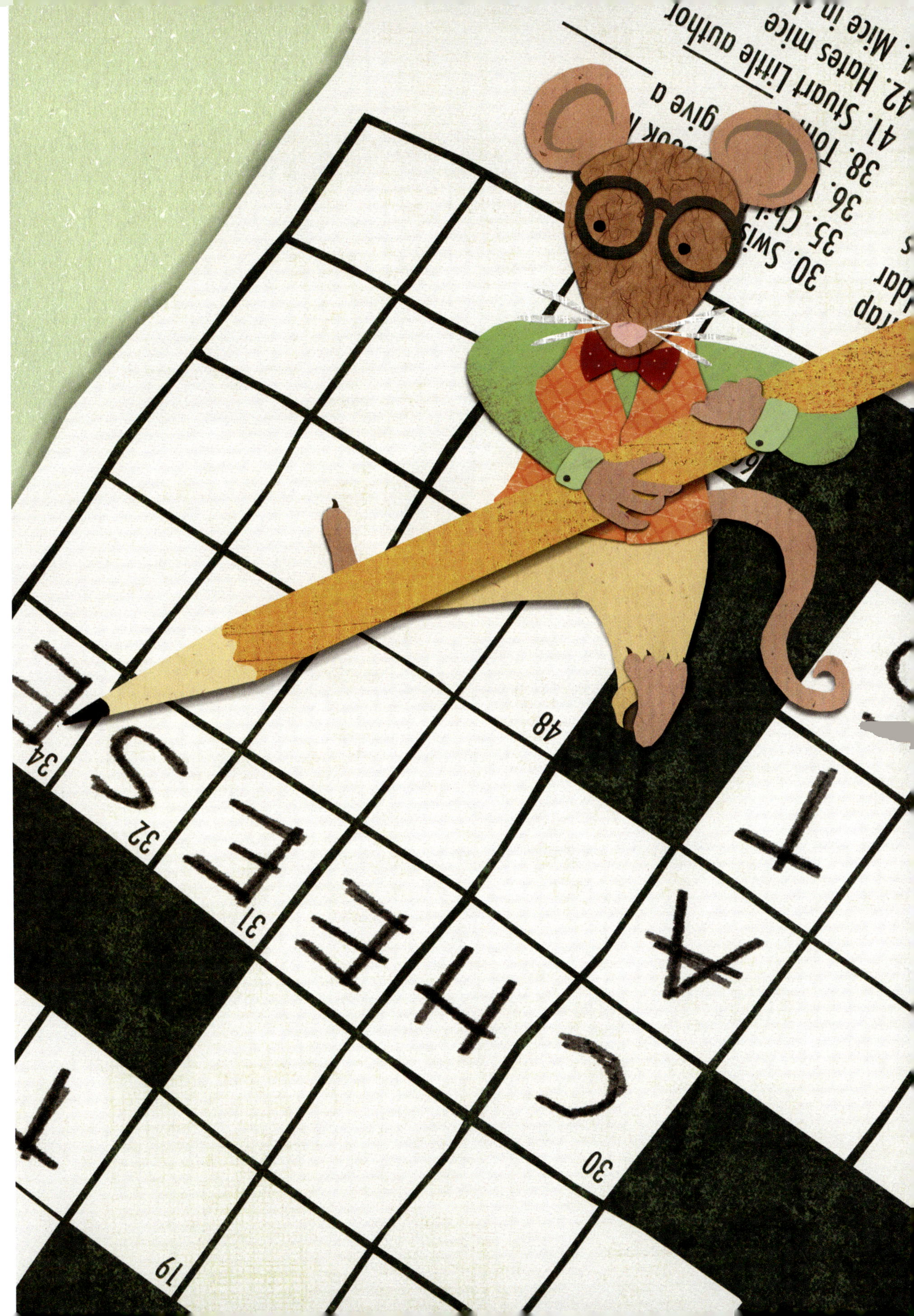
41. Stuart Little author
42. Hates mice

Read a rebus

Say the word for each picture and you have a rebus. A rebus is a puzzle with pictures for some words.

👁 🪚 a 🐱 go up a 🌳.

The 🐱 in the 🌳 🪚 me!

Sometimes a rebus uses a letter of the alphabet for a word. Read the letter aloud, and it sounds like a word:

I C U
I   see   you

Here are some two-letter combinations that sound like words. Just read the letters aloud, quickly:

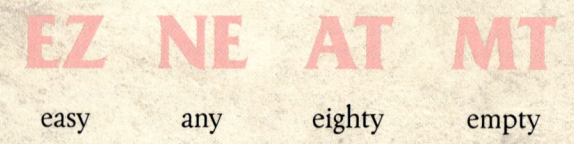

EZ NE AT MT
easy   any   eighty   empty

188 Letters to Words

A rebus may also use a number for a word.

1   **2**   **4**   **8**

won   to, too   for   ate

A number can also be part of a word:

1 + derful = wonderful

2 + day = today

Have you ever seen a text message that somebody sent on a cell phone? Usually, people abbreviate words to make the message as short as possible. They probably don't even realize that their message is like a rebus! See if you can understand the text message below:

RUOK? Y HAVEN'T I HERD FROM U 2DAY? MY TEST WAS EZ. I THINK I DID GR8! DO U WANT TO ET L8R? CU

Fun with Words

The riddle of the terrible Sphinx

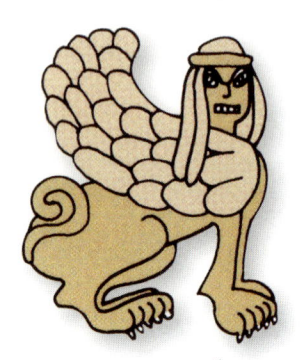

The horrible monster lay on a rock near the top of the mountain.
It waited, silently.
Who would be its next victim?

This terrible beast was the Sphinx. It had the head of a woman, the body of a lion, the wings of a bird, and the tail of a serpent. The Sphinx had eaten hundreds of people on their way to the nearby city of Thebes. And all because these people could not answer the riddle the cunning Sphinx had asked them.

Suddenly, the Sphinx raised its head.
SOMEONE WAS COMING!
Its sharp claws began to

open and close,
open and close.

A man drew near. He was about to pass, when the Sphinx leaped in front of him.

Letters to Words

The Sphinx said, *I will let you pass safely if you can answer my riddle.* The man, whose name was Oedipus, trembled. If he could not answer the riddle, he would be torn apart and eaten. But he knew he had no choice.

What is your riddle?

The monster's smile was cruel. "What is it that walks on four legs, then on two legs, and finally on three legs?"

Oedipus thought for a long while. The Sphinx began to circle about him. It moved closer and closer, ready to pounce. Nobody knew the answer to its riddle—nobody.

Finally, Oedipus replied. "The answer is 'man.' He crawls on all fours as a baby, then learns to walk on two legs, and finally needs a cane in his old age."

The furious Sphinx howled with rage. Oedipus had answered the riddle correctly! The howls grew louder and louder. Then, with a last, terrible SCREAM, the monster flung itself off the mountain to its death on the rocks below.

Fun with Words

Read a riddle

Long ago, people took riddles very seriously. The riddle of the Sphinx is one of the oldest and best-known riddles of all. Like all riddles, it's a puzzle with a hidden meaning that must be thought out or guessed.

Today, most riddles are silly questions with silly answers. The answers are a play on words that usually make people laugh—or at least smile or groan. See how often you laugh, smile, or groan when you learn the answers to these riddles:

1. What letter of the alphabet is:
   a. in your head?
   b. a small, round, green vegetable?

2. What has 18 legs and catches flies?

3. Why isn't your nose 12 inches long?

4. When does a doctor get mad?

5. What part of your body is:
   a. part of a clock?
   b. bent macaroni?
   c. corn on the cob?
   d. a young cow?
   e. the edge of a saw?

6. What tree:
   a. cries a lot?
   b. does everyone carry in their hands?

192 Letters to Words

Word games

Calling All Cities!

The leader calls out the name of any big city. The next player must name another city before the leader can count to 10. The name of this city must start with the last letter in the name of the city just called. Otherwise, the player is out. The winner is the last remaining player.

Word Snap!

The leader needs two or more sets of alphabet cards. The leader calls out a category, such as animals, and holds up one of the alphabet cards. The first player to call out an animal name that begins with the letter shown gets the card. The winner is the player who ends up with the most cards.

Fun with Words   193

Running back again

"Otto, the pup," said Mom, "has lots of pep at noon!"

How many palindromes can you find in that sentence? The word *palindrome* comes from a Greek word and means "running back again." So, a palindrome is a word, a group of words, or a sentence that is the same whether you read it backward or forward. That's the fun of a palindrome. The first sentence has five palindromes: Otto, pup, Mom, pep, and noon.

Here are some famous palindromes. They make as much sense when you read them backward as they do when you read them forward:

MADAM, I'M ADAM.

A MAN, A PLAN, A CANAL—PANAMA!

NAME NO ONE MAN

Letters to Words

Directions: The list of one-word palindromes appears in the palindrome puzzle. They appear not only forward and backward, but also up, down, and diagonally. Copy the puzzle on a sheet of ruled paper. Then find and mark the palindromes, as shown. Two palindromes appear more than once. Can you find them?

P	E	P	H	E	Y	E	S	E	E
A	K	C	U	A	S	A	H	A	M
L	O	E	V	E	N	A	N	S	O
I	O	A	E	T	B	N	D	I	R
N	K	S	G	O	A	D	A	L	D
D	W	E	B	T	I	N	D	H	N
R	Y	E	F	T	O	O	T	A	I
O	F	S	M	O	M	O	O	N	L
M	P	U	P	P	Y	N	I	N	A
E	M	O	R	D	N	I	L	A	P

PEP	EYE	SEES	NOON	MOM	DAD
NAN	ADA	EVE	ASA	BOB	OTTO
AVA	ANNA	PUP	TOOT	KOOK	HANNAH

Fun with Words **195**

Scrambled names

Here are three sets of scrambled names. Get a pencil and paper and copy the words. See how long it takes you to unscramble them.

The scrambled days and months should be easy. But the scrambled cities are harder. Some of the cities may stump you. If you have a problem unscrambling the cities, you'll find the answers on page 201.

Scrambled days

1. STUDYEA
2. RUTHYADS
3. TUAARYDS
4. AYSNUD
5. AFRDYI
6. YNMODA
7. DEEDSWAYN

Scrambled months

1. PLAIR
2. RAYBEURF
3. HARCM
4. REEDBECM
5. YARNJUA
6. ENJU
7. ROVMEBEN
8. ROOTBEC
9. ATSUGU
10. PEERSMETB
11. AYM
12. LUYJ

Scrambled cities

1. ICHOGCA
2. NODLNO
3. RASPI
4. MORE
5. RUNFAFKTR
6. YESNDY
7. YOOTK
8. ROOTNOT

Letters to Words

Categories

To play this game, make copies of the chart shown, one for each player.

The players write in names for each category. Each name must start with the letter shown at the top of the column. For example, when the animal category is complete, it might read *squirrel, monkey, impala, lion,* and *elephant*.

Players have up to 10 minutes to fill in the form. The winner is the first one to fill in the boxes correctly. You can change the game by using different categories and a different word at the top.

Category \ Word	S	M	I	L	E
Animal					
City					
Flower					
Food					
Famous People					

Fun with Words

Story crossword puzzle

This crossword puzzle contains words you have read in the five stories in this book: *The Journey of Gilgamesh, Beowulf and Grendel, Chauntecleer and the Fox, Nick Bottom and the Fairies,* and *Christmas at the Cratchits'.* Trace the puzzle onto a sheet of paper. Be sure to mark in the numbers you see in the boxes. Then, find a word that fits the spaces using the listed clues.

Down

1. Gilgamesh lived in the land of _____.
3. English author Dickens's first name
4. Beowulf is an epic _____.
5. The name of the sun god who helped Gilgamesh
6. On top of his head, Chauntecleer had a _____.
8. When the fox grabbed him, instead of panicking, Chauntecleer remained _____.
9. What country was Beowulf from?
11. Chauntecleer was carried off by a _____.
12. The legend of Gilgamesh was known by the people of _____.
14. What kind of animal was Pertelote?
16. Humbaba's gaze turned men into _____.
19. Puck gave Bottom the head of an _____.

Across

2. Mr. Cratchit and Tiny Tim had been at _____.
4. Shakespeare wrote many _____.
6. The monster Humbaba lived on the Mountain of the _____ Forest.
7. To protect himself, Beowulf wore _____.
8. Bob Cratchit was a _____.
10. The hero of the first great work in English literature
13. One of Titania's servants is named _____.
15. What weapon was useless against Grendel?
17. The youngest Cratchit was named_____.
18. Beowulf was a _____ to his people.
19. Ishtar's father's name
20. What did the Cratchits have for Christmas dinner?

Fun with Words   **199**

Answers to puzzles

page 188—Rebus

I saw a cat go up a tree. The cat in the tree saw me.

Text message (page 189): Are you o.k.? Why haven't I heard from you today? My test was easy. I think I did great! Do you want to eat later? See you

page 192—Read a riddle

1a. I (eye)
 b. P (pea)
2. a baseball team
3. because then it would be a foot
4. when he runs out of patients
5a. hand
 b. elbow
 c. ear
 d. calf
 e. teeth
6a. weeping willow
 b. palm tree

page 195—Running back again

P	E	P	H	E	Y	E	S	E	E
A	K	C	U	A	S	A	H	A	M
L	O	E	V	E	N	A	N	S	O
I	O	A	E	T	B	N	D	I	R
N	K	S	G	O	A	D	A	L	D
D	W	E	B	T	I	N	D	H	N
R	Y	E	F	T	O	O	T	A	I
O	F	S	M	O	M	O	O	N	L
M	P	U	P	P	Y	N	I	N	A
E	M	O	R	D	N	I	L	A	P

200   Letters to Words

page 196—Scrambled names

Scrambled days
1. Tuesday
2. Thursday
3. Saturday
4. Sunday
5. Friday
6. Monday
7. Wednesday

Scrambled months
1. April
2. February
3. March
4. December
5. January
6. June
7. November
8. October
9. August
10. September
11. May
12. July

Scrambled cities:
1. Chicago
2. London
3. Paris
4. Rome
5. Frankfurt
6. Sydney
7. Tokyo
8. Toronto

page 199—Story crossword puzzle

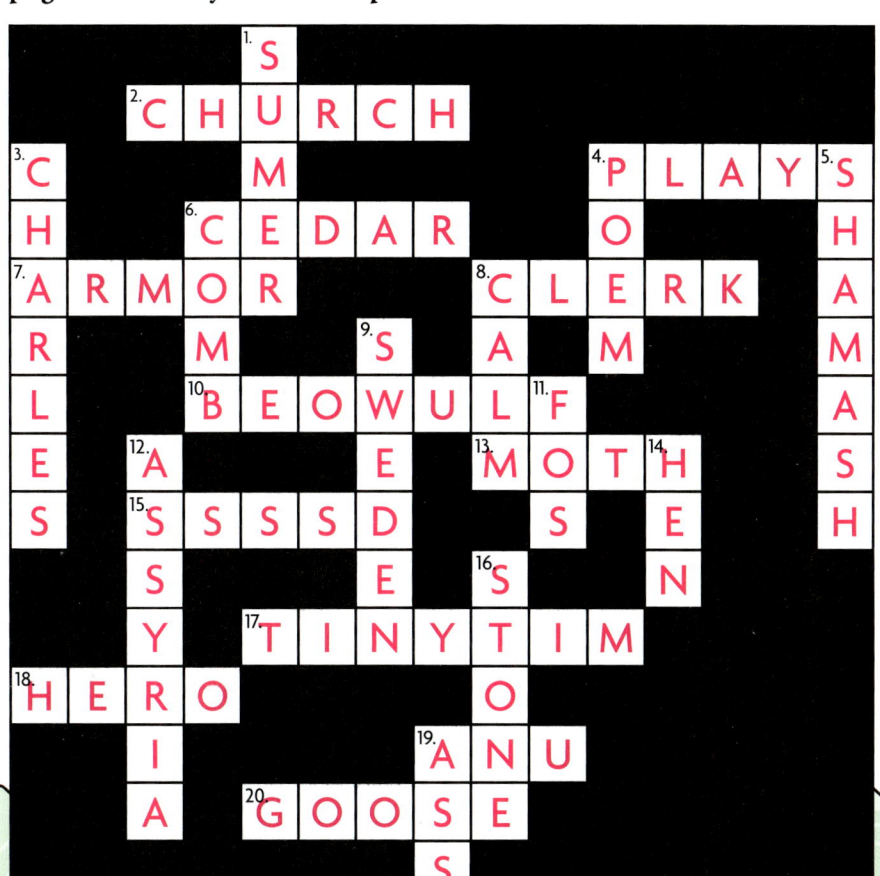

			1. S						
	2. C	H	U	R	C	H			
3. C			M				4. P	L	A	Y	5. S
H		6. C	E	D	A	R		O			H
7. A	R	M	O	R		8. C	L	E	R	K	A
R		M		9. S		A		M			M
L		10. B	E	O	W	U	L	F			A
E	12. A			E		13. M	O	T	H	14. H	S
S	15. S	S	S	S	D		S			E	H
	S			E		16. S				N	
	Y		17. T	I	N	Y	T	I	M		
18. H	E	R	O			O					
	I				19. A	N	U				
	A		20. G	O	O	S	E				
						S					

201

Find Out More

Books to read

Ages 3 to 5

Fanciful alphabets, funny riddles, and attractive illustrations introduce children to letters, sounds, and word meanings.

ABC by Dr. Seuss (Collins, 2005)

A Is for Art: An Abstract Alphabet by Stephen Johnson (Simon & Schuster Books for Young Readers, 2008)

LMNO Peas by Keith Baker (Beach Lane Books, 2010)

Peter Rabbit's Hide and Seek ABC by Beatrix Potter (Frederick Warne, 2004)

Richard Scarry's Find Your ABC's by Richard Scarry (Sterling, 2008)

Sign Language ABC by Lora Heller (Sterling, 2012)

Welcome to My Neighborhood: A Barrio ABC by Quiara Alegría Hudes and Shino Arihara (Arthur A. Levine Books, 2010)

What Do You Hear When Cows Sing? And Other Silly Riddles by Marco Maestro and Giulio Maestro (HarperCollins Publishers, 1996)

Ages 5 to 8

The Dangerous Alphabet by Neil Gaiman and Gris Grimly (HarperCollins Publishers, 2008)
Two children and their pet gazelle travel through an alphabet full of monsters.

The Dove Dove: Funny Homograph Riddles by Marvin Terban and Tom Huffman (Clarion Books, 2008)
Homographs create hilarious puzzles for readers.

Oh Say Can You Say? by Dr. Seuss (Beginner Books, 1979)
A classic collection of tongue twisters in verse by a beloved children's author

Sparkle and Spin: A Book About Words by Ann Rand and Paul Rand (Chronicle Books, 2006)
Playful artwork and lyrical text reveal the magic of words; an updated version of a classic.

The Z Was Zapped: A Play in 26 Acts by Chris Van Allsburg (Houghton Mifflin Company, 1998)
26 letters live out 26 dramatic—and alliterative—fates in this book of "alphabet theater."

Ages 9 to 12

The Everything Kids' More Word Searches Puzzle and Activity Book by Beth L. Blair and Jennifer A. Ericsson (Adams Media, 2010)
Word games, puzzles, rebuses, and secret codes fill this activity book with fun.

The Mystery of the Hieroglyphs: The Story of the Rosetta Stone and the Race to Decipher Egyptian Hieroglyphs by Carol Donoughue (Oxford University Press, 1999)
Explains the writing system of ancient Egypt and how the discovery of the Rosetta stone unlocked the mysteries of some ancient languages

Ox, House, Stick: The History of our Alphabet by Don Robb and Anne Smith (Charlesbridge, 2007)
Traces the history of our modern alphabet to its roots in the ancient world; illuminates both the development of each letter and the spread of different writing systems

Pun and Games: Jokes, Riddles, Daffynitions, Tairy Fales, Rhymes and More Wordplay for Kids by Richard Lederer and Dave Morice (Chicago Review Press, 1996)
An introduction to clever wordplay full of hilarious examples; readers learn to design their own jokes, riddles, and puns

Top Secret: A Handbook of Codes, Ciphers, and Secret Writing by Paul B. Janeczko and Jenna La Reau (Candlewick Press, 2006)
Reveals the long and fascinating history of secret writing while challenging readers to come up with their own uncrackable codes

The Word Snoop by Ursula Dubosarsky and Tohby Riddle (Dial Books, 2009)
Follows the history of the English language from the earliest alphabets to modern slang and text-speak; activities include anagrams, codes, and puzzles

Websites to visit

A, B, C, Alphabet Games
http://pbskids.org/games/alphabet.html
Alphabet match-ups, paint by letter, and letter-of-the-day games at this site by PBS Kids

Alphabet Games
http://www.playkidsgames.com/alphabetGames.htm
Students can play around with letters, words, and alphabetical order at this educational game site.

Funbrain
http://www.funbrain.com/words.html
Word games for various reading levels at this site for children, parents, and educators

Learning Games: Homophones
http://www.learninggamesforkids.com/vocabulary_games/homophones-games.html
The games at this website provide practice with homophones—words that sound alike but are spelled differently and have different meanings.

Primary Games: Crossword Puzzle
http://www.primarygames.com/langarts/crosswordpuzzle/start.htm
This online crossword will help students exercise their vocabulary and spelling skills.

Index

This index is an alphabetical list of important topics covered in this book. It will help you find information given in both words and pictures. To help you understand what an entry means, there is sometimes a helping word in parentheses, for example, **Celts** (people). If there is information in both words and pictures, you will see the words *with pictures* in parentheses after the page number. If there is only a picture, you will see the word *picture* in parentheses after the page number.

A

a (letter), 46 *(pictures)*
accents. *See* **dialects**
Africa, 164
Akkadian language, 13 *(picture)*
alphabet, 8
  English, 42-45
  Gaelic, 72-73 *(picture)*
  Greek, 34-36 *(with pictures),* 70-71 *(picture)*
  Hebrew, 72-73 *(picture)*
  Phoenician, 32-36 *(with pictures),* 70-71 *(picture)*
  Roman, 37-39 *(with pictures),* 70-71 *(picture)*
  Russian, 72-73 *(picture)*
  Semitic, 30-31 *(with pictures),* 70-71 *(picture)*
  see also individual letters
Angles (people), 130-131, 138
Anglo-Saxons (people)
  Beowulf (story), 133
  language of, 131, 132, 144, 174
animals
  last names from, 122-123
  names of, 80-82 *(with pictures)*
Arabia, 163
astronaut (word), 105
attic (word), 84 *(with picture)*
Australia
  dialect of, 183
  spellings in, 184
  word meanings in, 179-181
Australian Aborigines, 164, 180, 181
Aztec Indians, 164

B

b (letter), 47 *(pictures)*
baker (word), 117 *(with picture)*
barber (word), 92 *(with picture)*
Behistun Rock (Iran), 14 *(with picture)*
Beowulf (poem), 133-137 *(with pictures),* 198
biofuel (word), 103, 104
birds, last names from, 122-123
book (word), 90-91 *(with picture)*
breakfast (word), 86 *(with picture)*
Britannia (island), 128-131 *(with pictures)*
Britons (people), 130-131 *(with picture)*
bus (word), 100-101 *(with picture)*

C

c (letter), 48 *(pictures)*
cab (word), 101 *(with picture)*
Calling All Cities! (game), 193
Canada, 183-184
Canterbury Tales, The (poem), 147-153 *(with pictures),* 198
capital letters, 40 *(with picture)*
Caribbean Islands, 164
categories (game), 197
Celts (people), 128-130 *(with picture)*
Champollion, Jean-François (historian), 27-28 *(with picture)*
Chaucer, Geoffrey (poet), 147
Chauntecleer and the Fox (story), 148-153 *(with pictures),* 198
China, 163
Christianity, 138-139
Christmas at the Cratchits' (story), 166-173 *(with pictures),* 198
Christmas Carol, A (book), 165-173 *(with pictures),* 198

204 Letters to Words

cleric (word), 92-93 *(with picture)*
clerk (word), 93 *(with picture)*
cockneys (people), 181, 183
coleslaw (word), 76-77
consonants, 31, 34, 43
crocodile (word), 80 *(with picture)*
crossword puzzle, 198-199 *(with picture)*
cuneiform writing, 10-13 *(with pictures),* 29
   learning to read, 14 *(with pictures),* 16
cursive script, 40
cut-off words, 100-101

D
d (letter), 49 *(pictures)*
Darius (king of Persia), 14 *(with pictures)*
dialects, 182-183
Dickens, Charles (author), 165
   A Christmas Carol, 165-173 *(with pictures),* 198
dinner (word), 87 *(with picture)*
dinosaur (word), 82
duck (word), 81 *(with picture)*
dungarees (word), 89

E
e (letter), 50-51 *(pictures)*
Egyptians, ancient, 24-25 *(with pictures)*
   see also **hieroglyphics**
Elizabeth I (queen of England), 154
Elizabethan Age, 154, 162
engineer (word), 94-95 *(with picture)*
England, 42, 83, 84
   Anglo-Saxon rule, 130-131
   Christianity in, 138-139
   dialects in, 182, 183
   Elizabethan Age in, 154, 162
   Norman conquest of, 42, 142-143
   Roman rule, 128-129 *(with picture)*
   spellings in, 184-185
   Viking invasions of, 140-141
   word meanings in, 178-181
English language
   alphabet, development of, 42-45
   as world language, 174-175
   dialects in, 182-183
   French words in, 88-89, 143-146, 162, 174
   in Elizabethan Age, 154, 162
   Latin words in, 139
   Norse words in, 141
   origins, 124, 131
   spelling differences in, 184-185
   word meaning differences in, 178-181
   words from everywhere in, 162-164, 174
   see also **Middle English; Old English;** *and individual letters of the alphabet*
Ethelbert (king), 138-139
Etruscans (people), 37

F
f (letter), 52 *(pictures)*
fan (word), 102 *(with picture)*
first names, 106, 108-111
   last names from, 114-115
fish (word), **spelling of,** 184
food names, 76-79 *(with pictures)*
football (word), 178
France
   lower-case letters in, 40-41 *(with picture)*
   Norman conquest, 42, 142-143
   see also **French language; Normans**
French fries (term), 78 *(with picture)*
French language
   English words from, 88-89, 96, 100-102, 143-146, 162, 174
   letters in, 42-44 *(with pictures)*

G
g (letter), 53 *(pictures)*
Gaelic alphabet, 72-73 *(picture)*
General American accent, 182
Germany, 77, 81
Giffey, George (merchant), 79
Gilgamesh legend, 16-23 *(with pictures),* 198
Greeks, ancient, 34-36 *(with pictures),* 70-71 *(picture)*
   hieroglyphics and, 24, 28
   Roman alphabet and, 37, 39, 40
   word origins and, 80, 82, 84, 90, 103
grocer (word), 95 *(with picture)*
gun (word), 102 *(with picture)*

H
h (letter), 53 *(pictures)*
hamburger (word), 76-77 *(with picture)*

Hebrew alphabet, 72-73 *(picture)*
hieroglyphics, 24-25 *(with pictures)*
   difficulty in writing, 29-30 *(with picture)*
   invention of alphabet and, 30
   learning to read, 26-28
hippopotamus (word), 74, 80 *(with picture)*

I
i (letter), 44 *(with picture)*, 54 *(pictures)*
India, 163
Indians, American, 82, 115, 164
Inuit, 164
invented words, 103-105
Iran, 14-15 *(with pictures)*, 163
Italy, 37, 43, 162, 163

J
j (letter), 39, 44, 55 *(pictures)*
Japan, 163
jeans (word), 88-89 *(with pictures)*
jeggings (pants), 89 *(with picture)*
jobs
   last names from, 116-117
   names of, 92-95 *(with pictures)*
Journey of Gilgamesh, The (story), 16-23 *(with pictures)*, 198
Jutes (people), 130-131

K
k (letter), 56 *(pictures)*
Kadmus (prince), 34
ketchup (word), 78 *(with picture)*
kitchen (word), 85

L
l (letter), 44, 57 *(pictures)*
language, origin of, 126-127
last names, 106, 112-113
   from animals, 122-123
   from first names, 114-115
   from jobs, 116-117
   from nicknames, 118-119
   from places, 120-121
Latin language, 37-39 *(with pictures)*, 44, 174
   in England, 129, 130, 139
   word origins and, 91, 92, 96, 101
   See also **Romans**

letters. See **alphabet; writing**
Levi's (jeans), 88, 89
Lord's Prayer, The, 132
lower-case letters, 40 *(with picture)*
lunch (word), 86 *(with picture)*

M
m (letter), 58 *(pictures)*
mail carrier (term), 94 *(with picture)*
Malaya, 163
meals, names of, 86-87 *(with pictures)*
Megalosaurus (dinosaur), 82
metalworkers, names of, 116
Middle English (language), 97, 146, 147
Midsummer Night's Dream, A (play), 155-161 *(with pictures)*, 198
moose (word), 82 *(with picture)*

N
n (letter), 58 *(pictures)*
names, 74
   animals, 80-82 *(with pictures)*
   food, 76-79 *(with pictures)*
   houses, parts of, 83-85 *(with pictures)*
   jobs, 92-95 *(with pictures)*
   meals, 86-87 *(with pictures)*
   pants and related words, 88-89 *(with pictures)*
   school and things relating to school, 90-91 *(with pictures)*
   scrambled (puzzle), 196
   see also **personal names; words**
naughty (word), 96-97
Netherlands, The, 77, 163
New England, 182-183
nice (word), 96
Nick Bottom and the Fairies (story), 156-161 *(with pictures)*, 198
nicknames, 118-119, 122
Norman-French (language). See **Normans**
Normans (people)
   conquest of England, 142-143 *(with picture)*
   language of, 42, 144-146, 174
Norsemen. See **Vikings**

O
o (letter), 59 *(pictures)*
octopus (word), 82 *(with picture)*

Old English (language), 116, 146, 174
  beginnings, 131
  Beowulf story in, 133
  letters in, 42-43
  words from, 81, 90, 97, 132, 144
Old French (language), 42, 144-145
omnibus (word), 100-101

P

p (letter), 59 *(pictures)*
palindromes (games), 194-195 *(with pictures)*
Pantalone (character), 88
pants (word), 88-89 *(with pictures)*
paper, invention of, 25
parchment, 40
pen (word), 91 *(with picture)*
pencil (word), 91 *(with picture)*
Persia. *See* **Iran**
personal names, 106
  see also **first names; last names**
Phoenicians (people), 32-36 *(with pictures),* 70-71 *(picture)*
photograph (word), 104
pictograms, 10
  see also **cuneiform writing; hieroglyphics**
Picts (people), 130-131
poodle (word), 81 *(with picture)*
Portugal, 163
pronunciation
  changes in English, 132, 146, 154
  dialects and, 182-183
pupil (word), 91 *(with picture)*

Q

q (letter), 60-61 *(pictures)*
quick (word), 97

R

r (letter), 62 *(pictures)*
Rawlinson, Henry (army officer), 14-15
rebus (puzzle), 188-189 *(with pictures)*
riddles, 190-192 *(with pictures)*
Romans
  alphabet of, 37-40 *(with pictures),* 70-71 *(picture)*
  English words from, 84, 138-139, 174
  rule of Britain by, 128-129 *(with picture)*
  see also **Latin language**

roof (word), 85 *(with picture)*
Rosetta stone, 28 *(with picture)*
Russia, 72-73 *(picture),* 163

S

s (letter), 63 *(pictures)*
sandwich (word), 76-77 *(with picture)*
Sandwich, Earl of (nobleman), 77
Saxons (people), 130-131, 138, 146
  conquest by Normans, 142-143
  language of, 144-145
school words, 90-91 *(with pictures)*
Scots (people), 130-131
scrambled names (puzzle), 196
Semites (people), 30-31 *(with pictures),* 70-71 *(picture)*
Shakespeare, William (author), 154 *(with picture)*
  A Midsummer Night's Dream, 155-161 *(with pictures),* 198
silly (word), 97
slang, 180-181
smith (word), 116 *(with picture)*
soccer (word), 178
sounds
  in Greek language, 34-36
  language origins in, 126-127
  symbols representing, 8, 30-31
  words imitating, 98-99
Spain, 44, 162, 163
spelling, 184-185
Sphinx, Riddle of the, 190-192 *(with pictures)*
spider (word), 81 *(with picture)*
Strauss, Levi (merchant), 89
Sumerians, 10-13 *(with pictures),* 25
  Gilgamesh legend, 16-23 *(with pictures)*
  understanding language of, 14-15 *(with pictures)*
sundae (word), 78-79 *(with picture)*
supper (word), 87 *(with picture)*
swagman (word), 180-181 *(with picture)*

T

t (letter), 63 *(pictures)*
tailor (word), 117 *(with picture)*
telephone (word), 103, 104
teller (word), 93 *(with picture)*

U

u (letter), 39, 42-43, 64-65 *(pictures)*
United Kingdom, 83, 128
    dialects in, 182-183
    spellings in, 184-185
    word meanings in, 178-181
    see also **England**
United States
    dialects in, 182-183
    spellings in, 184-185
    word meanings in, 178-181

V

v (letter), 39, 42-43 *(with picture)*, 66 *(pictures)*
Vikings (people), 83, 140-141 *(with picture)*, 174
villain (word), 96-97
Vortigern (king of the Britons), 130-131
vowels, 31, 34-36, 43

W

w (letter), 39, 42-43, 67 *(pictures)*
wall (word), 84
"Waltzing Matilda" (song), 180-181 *(with picture)*
William the Conqueror (king of England), 142-143
window (word), 83-84 *(with picture)*
word games, 186, 193 *(with pictures)*
words
    changes in meanings of, 96-97
    countries and choice of, 178-181
    cuneiform, 10-15 *(with pictures)*, 29
    cut-off, 100-101
    Elizabethan English, 154
    hieroglyphic, 29 *(with picture)*
    imitating sounds, 98-99
    in Dickens, 165
    invented, 103-105
    Middle English, 147
    Old English, 132
    pronunciation of, 182-183
    representing sounds, 30
    scrambled (game), 196
    spellings of, 184-185
    see also **English language**; **names**
Word Snap! (game), 193
work. *See* **jobs**
writing, 8
    capital and lower-case letters in, 40-41 *(with picture)*
    Greek, 34-36 *(with pictures)*
    Phoenician, 32-33 *(with pictures)*
    Roman, 37-40 *(with pictures)*
    Sumerian, 10-15 *(with pictures)*
    see also **alphabet**; **cuneiform writing**; **hieroglyphics**

X

X (letter), 67 *(pictures)*

Y

Y (letter), 68 *(pictures)*

Z

Z (letter), 69 *(pictures)*